Cambridge Elements

Elements in Development Economics
Series Editor-in-Chief
Kunal Sen
UNU-WIDER and University of Manchester

FINANCING FOR DEVELOPMENT

The Global Agenda

José Antonio Ocampo
Columbia University

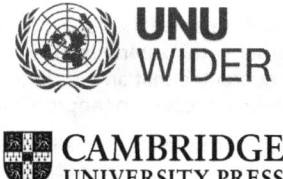

Shaftesbury Road, Cambridge CB2 8EA, United Kingdom

One Liberty Plaza, 20th Floor, New York, NY 10006, USA

477 Williamstown Road, Port Melbourne, VIC 3207, Australia

314–321, 3rd Floor, Plot 3, Splendor Forum, Jasola District Centre, New Delhi – 110025, India

103 Penang Road, #05–06/07, Visioncrest Commercial, Singapore 238467

Cambridge University Press is part of Cambridge University Press & Assessment, a department of the University of Cambridge.

We share the University's mission to contribute to society through the pursuit of education, learning and research at the highest international levels of excellence.

www.cambridge.org
Information on this title: www.cambridge.org/9781009613385

DOI: 10.1017/9781009613330

© UNU-WIDER 2025

This publication is in copyright. Subject to statutory exception and to the provisions of relevant collective licensing agreements, with the exception of the Creative Commons version the link for which is provided below, no reproduction of any part may take place without the written permission of Cambridge University Press & Assessment.

An online version of this work is published at doi.org/10.1017/9781009613330 under a Creative Commons Open Access license CC-BY-NC-SA 3.0 IGO which permits re-use, distribution and reproduction in any medium for non-commercial purposes providing appropriate credit to the original work is given, any changes made are indicated, and the new work is published under the same licence terms. When the licensor is an intergovernmental organisation, disputes will be resolved by mediation and arbitration where possible. To view a copy of this license, visit https://creativecommons.org/licenses/by-nc-sa/3.0/igo

When citing this work, please include a reference to the DOI 10.1017/9781009613330

First published 2025

A catalogue record for this publication is available from the British Library

ISBN 978-1-009-61338-5 Hardback
ISBN 978-1-009-61337-8 Paperback
ISSN 2755-1601 (online)
ISSN 2755-1598 (print)

Cambridge University Press & Assessment has no responsibility for the persistence or accuracy of URLs for external or third-party internet websites referred to in this publication and does not guarantee that any content on such websites is, or will remain, accurate or appropriate.

For EU product safety concerns, contact us at Calle de José Abascal, 56, 1°, 28003 Madrid, Spain, or email eugpsr@cambridge.org.

Financing for Development

The Global Agenda

Elements in Development Economics

DOI: 10.1017/9781009613330
First published online: March 2025

José Antonio Ocampo
Columbia University

Author for correspondence: José Antonio Ocampo,
ocampo.joseantonio@yahoo.com

Abstract: The reform of the international financial and tax systems has been at the center of global debates in recent years – in the United Nations, the World Bank, the International Monetary Fund (IMF), the OECD, and the G20. The fourth United Nations Conference on Financing for Development that will take place in Spain in 2025 also represents a great opportunity to enhance global cooperation in this area. This Element analyzes six elements of the global financing for development agenda, which are dealt with in individual sections: the role and evolution of development financing, the international monetary system, sovereign debt restructuring, international tax cooperation, international trade, and critical institutional issues. Although focusing on the international agenda, many of these issues have domestic implications for developing countries. The analysis covers both the nature of cooperation and recommendations on how to improve it. This title is also available as Open Access on Cambridge Core.

Keywords: international cooperation, development, international finance, tax cooperation, United Nations

© UNU-WIDER 2025

ISBNs: 9781009613385 (HB), 9781009613378 (PB), 9781009613330 (OC)
ISSNs: 2755-1601 (online), 2755-1598 (print)

Contents

Introduction 1

1 Multilateral Development Banks 2

2 The International Monetary System 14

3 Sovereign Debt Restructuring 25

4 International Tax Cooperation 34

5 International Trade 41

6 Critical Institutional Issues 48

References 54

Financing for Development 1

Introduction

The reform of the international financial and tax systems has been at the center of recent global debates. The United Nations Secretary General has proposed a stimulus to achieve the sustainable development goals (SDGs) and broader suggestions on international financial reforms (UN, 2023a, 2023b and 2024a). Many of these proposals were endorsed in the political declaration of the High-Level Political Forum on Sustainable Development held in September 2023 (UN, 2023c, paragraph 38). There have been additional contributions in 2024 from the United Nations (2024a), in particular the recommendations of the Economic and Social Council (ECOSOC) Forum on Financing for Development (UN, 2024b), as well as from the Bretton Woods Institutions and the Group of 20 (G20) and academic institutions.[1] The United Nations Pact for the Future also included an important set of "Actions" to both enhance financing for development and adopt the associated relevant reforms in global governance (UN, 2024d).[2] These issues have also been at the center of the agenda of the Financing for Development Conferences since Monterrey in 2002, in those of the G20 and the Bretton Woods Institutions, as well as in recurring debates, including on the equitable participation of developing countries[3] in international economic decision-making.

The celebration of the eightieth anniversary of the Bretton Woods Institutions in 2024, the G20 meetings in Brazil in 2024 and South Africa in 2025, and the negotiations on international tax cooperation going on in the United Nations constitute opportunities to make additional contributions to this agenda. In turn, the fourth Conference on Financing for Development that will take place in Spain in 2025 represents a great opportunity to enhance global cooperation in this area. It should follow the Addis Ababa Action Agenda agreed in the third Conference that took place in 2015 (United Nations, 2015). In this Conference, the United Nations should serve as a forum for consensus building – no doubt its historical strength – but the agreed financing actions should be in the hands of the appropriate financial institutions and other international financial arrangements.

In this Element, I refer to six elements of the global financing for development agenda, which are dealt with in individual sections: the role and evolution

---

[1] An interesting recent contribution is that of Brookings (2024), based on a consultation process with several analysts.
[2] See, in particular, the section on sustainable development and financing for development, and Actions 47–54 in the section on transforming global governance.
[3] These countries include the so-called emerging economies, a term that lacks a clear definition. I will always include them when referring in this Element to "developing countries," although the historical and even increasing heterogeneity of this large group of countries should of course be recognized.

of development financing, the international monetary system, sovereign debt restructuring, international tax cooperation, international trade, and critical institutional issues. Although focusing on the international agenda, many of these issues have domestic implications for developing countries. The analysis covers both the nature of cooperation and recommendations on how to improve it. The proposed reforms would help implement recent global agreements, particularly the Actions of the United Nations Pact for the Future.

This Element is a revised version of a report prepared for the United Nations Department of Economic and Social Affairs as a background for the forthcoming Conference on Financing for Development. I make use of multiple contributions to these debates, including my own, in several cases in collaboration with other authors. I thank Mariangela Parra-Lancourt and Shari Spiegel for her backing to this project. Support from Karla Daniela González has been crucial for the whole Element; Sections 1 and 3 borrow from joint papers written with her. I also appreciate the support of Juan Sebastián Betancur, Tommaso Faccio, Carlos Felipe Jaramillo, and Natalia Quiñonez for different sections.

1 Multilateral Development Banks

The system of multilateral development banks (MDBs) has its origins in the creation of the International Bank for Reconstruction and Development (IBRD) at the Bretton Woods Conference of 1944, which is today part of the World Bank Group (simply World Bank in the rest of the Element). In terms of development, financing was enriched in later years with the creation of the International Development Association (IDA), the International Finance Corporation (IFC), and the Multilateral Investment Guarantee Agency (MIGA). The system was later supplemented with the launch of several regional and interregional banks. Among the regional ones, the first were the European Investment Bank (EIB) and the Inter-American Development Bank (IDB), created in 1958 and 1959, respectively, followed later by the African Development Bank (AfDB), the Asian Development Bank (ADB), the Development Bank of Latin America (CAF),[4] and the European Bank for Reconstruction and Development (EBRD). The interregional institutions include the Islamic Development Bank (IsDB), to which two more institutions were added in the mid-2010s: the Asian Infrastructure Investment Bank (AIIB) and the New Development Bank (NDB) – the latter of the BRICS countries, but now with a broadening membership.

---

[4] This institution is the result of the transformation into a regional bank of the Andean Development Corporation, created in 1968. The institution kept is old Spanish acronym (CAF). It also includes now, as members, two European countries with historical links with Latin America, Spain, and Portugal.

The main purpose of these institutions was to provide development financing and, in some cases, support regional integration – the latter being a particularly important task assigned to the EIB when it was created. The need for public sector institutions was clearly in the origin of the earlier MDBs due to the negative effects that the Great Depression of the 1930s had had on international private financing, except for trade. Such private financing began to be rebuilt globally from the late 1950s and began to reach a group of developing countries in the late 1960s and early 1970s but remained limited or very costly for most of them. Access became broader after the 2007–9 North Atlantic financial crisis,[5] primarily encouraged by the very expansionary monetary policies that were put in place by major developed countries' central banks, which led to additional financing for developing nations that already had access to private international markets, as well as access to new countries that came to be characterized as "frontier markets."

In terms of support for developing countries, the MDBs were designed to finance basic public sector programs in countries with little access to private markets – virtually all of them until the 1960s, except for trade financing — and on more favorable conditions in terms of cost and maturities for those countries that do have access to the said markets. Funding was initially for projects but has subsequently extended to programs and broader budget support. Aside from the public sector, the MDBs also started to finance private investments, an activity that, in several cases, was assumed by financial corporations or similar entities that are part of the respective groups.

Several institutions have preferential lines for low-income countries, including through specialized entities, such as IDA in the World Bank. This task is complementary to other direct mechanisms of support to these countries through official development assistance, coordinated by the Development Assistance Committee of the Organization for Economic Cooperation and Development (OECD), and more recently by bilateral financing from other official countries – particularly from China.

We should add these historical functions, the countercyclical role that the MDBs must play, which is essential due to the procyclical behavior of international private financing toward developing countries –in terms of both availability and costs. Through their technical and financial support mechanisms, these institutions can help soften or reduce the negative impact of financial or economic crises, such as those triggered by COVID-19 and the restrictive monetary policies adopted by central banks in response to the increase in the global inflation generated by Russia's invasion of Ukraine in February 2022.

---

[5] I use this term to refer to this, generally called the Global Financial Crisis, since it centered in the United States and Western Europe and did not have a very strong effect on other regions of the world. This is why North Atlantic is a more appropriate name for this crisis.

Beyond these functions, the World Bank expanded its role to include technical assistance to individual countries and the analysis of the situation and appropriate policies for developing countries. This "knowledge bank" function, as it has sometimes been called, began with the creation of the Office of the Chief Economist in the 1970s. It has gradually been assumed by several other MDBs. The World Bank also began to perform functions associated with guaranteeing investments in developing countries through MIGA and providing for dispute resolutions between investors and sovereign states through the International Centre for Settlement of Investment Disputes (ICSID). In terms of public sector objectives, in recent years the emphasis has been added on financing international public goods, both global and regional, particularly mitigation and adaptation to climate change, supporting biodiversity and combating pandemics.

There are two basic models of MDBs. The first follows the original design of the IBRD, according to which there is a difference between borrowing and nonborrowing members, which are broadly speaking developing and developed countries, respectively. Everyone contributes capital and, in a certain sense, the subscribed but unpaid capital of the developed ones operates as a kind of financial guarantee, which helps to strengthen the institution and, therefore, its investment grade. The other model is the cooperative one. In this case, all countries are potential borrowers and equally share the risks faced by the institution. This is the model of the EIB and CAF but also of the interregional banks. Regarding the first of these models, it is important to mention that there is a complex debate about the "graduation" of countries, especially in the case of the World Bank. According to this criterion, above a certain level of income the country becomes developed and cannot borrow from the institution, although it could continue using a menu of options, especially the bank's advisory services.

According to Figure 1, financing from the MDBs to developing countries has increased over the past two decades – as a proportion of world GDP, from 0.14 percent in 2000 to 0.20 percent in 2022. However, as pointed out below in this section, financing is considered limited relative to the resources that should help finance current global demands by developing countries. Traditional regional banks that offer financing to developing countries (i.e., excluding the EIB[6]) have grown faster than the World Bank Group and surpass it in terms of loan commitments since the middle of the 2000s. Added to this is the growth of the two new banks, the AIIB and the NDB –particularly of the former – which was very rapid during the early years of its operation, in the second half of the 2010s.

---

[6] It should be pointed out that, aside from its support to the European Union countries, the EIB has historically supported Mediterranean countries and more recently developing countries from other regions.

Financing for Development 5

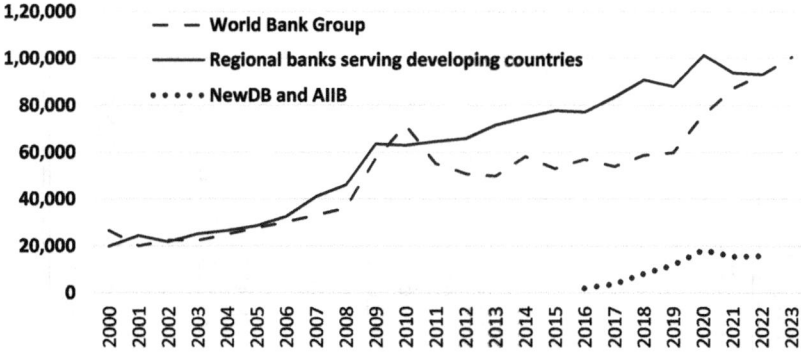

Figure 1 Loan commitments by Multilateral Development Banks (million dollars).
Source: Annual reports of each institution. For the World Bank Group, the data data refers to fiscal years.

Nonetheless, the World Bank continues to play the most important countercyclical role, as reflected in Figure 1 in the sharp increase in its financing during the North Atlantic and the COVID-19 crises, as well as the complex recent global economic conjuncture. The recent response was facilitated by the Bank's capitalization in 2018. Furthermore, in recent years, this function was performed more strongly by the IDA than by the IBRD, thus benefiting in particular low-income countries, but also with a significant increase in financing to middle-income nations by the second of these institutions (Table 1). The only traditional regional banks that played a significant countercyclical role during the pandemic were the ADB and the EBRD, while the two Latin American and Caribbean banks were not very dynamic and the AfDB reduced its credit approvals. Among the interregional banks, the one that played a stronger countercyclical role was the AIIB.

In terms of total financing, the World Bank has reached the size of the EIB, which was historically the largest development bank (see Table 1). Among the regional banks, the ADB is the largest, followed by the two Latin American and Caribbean banks (IDB and CAF), if we add the financing they provide. In the case of the interregional banks, the AIIB is now the largest.

In terms of relative support to different regions in relation to regional GDP, the World Bank provides the largest financing to Sub-Saharan Africa and South Asia. This clearly reflects the priority of supporting the world's poorest developing regions. Latin America and the Caribbean follow in relative importance. For its part, the support by regional banks is dominant in Europe, among other reasons due to importance of EIB, followed by Latin America and the Caribbean (Ocampo and Ortega, 2022).

Table 1 Loan commitments by Multilateral Development Banks (annual averages in million dollars)

	2000–2004	2005–2009	2010–2014	2015–2019	2020–2022
World Bank – IBRD	11,027	17,391	25,074	24,412	30,524
World Bank – IDA	8,896	11,060	16,822	20,118	34,707
International Finance Corporation – IFC	3,335	8,448	15,184	11,965	20,167
Subtotal World Bank Group	23,258	36,899	57,080	56,495	85,398
Inter-American Development Bank (IADB)	5,645	9,537	12,351	12,720	14,484
Development Bank of Latin America (CAF)	3,124	6,798	10,674	12,576	13,813
African Development Bank (AfDB)	2,190	3,916	4,702	7,029	4,944
Asian Development Bank (AsDB)	5,541	9,179	20,487	30,605	38,519
Asian Infraestucture Development Bank (AIDB)	–	–	–	2,037	10,444
New Development Bank (NewDB)	–	–	–	3,057	6,016
European Bank for Reconstruction and Development (EBRD)	3,749	7,531	11,575	12,175	15,562
Islamic Development Bank (IsDB)	3,307	5,369	8,161	8,373	8,744
Subtotal Regional Banks supporting developing countries	23,555	42,331	67,949	88,573	1,12,525
European Investment Bank (EIB)	46,900	87,871	98,044	84,423	84,966
TOTAL	93,714	1,67,101	2,23,073	2,29,490	2,82,889

Source: See Figure 1.

From this analysis, the importance of continued dynamism of the MDB system emerges, for both long-term financing, now including the fight against climate change and protecting biodiversity, and supporting countries during economic crises. As we will see below in this section, their support to both mitigation and adaptation to climate change has been increasing, but it is still small in relation to financing needs, and very limited in the case of biodiversity activities. In relation to support during crises, it is essential that regional banks also play a countercyclical role, complementing that of the World Bank.

Aside from the UN documents mentioned in the Introduction to this Element, there are recent ambitious proposals on the MDBs coming from the G20 independent expert groups on capital requirements (G20, 2022 and 2023a) and on the agenda of this institution (G20, 2023b), as well as in the World Bank's "Evolution Roadmap" (World Bank, 2022b, 2023b and 2024). The New Delhi G20 Summit also made ambitious proposals in this field (G20, 2023b, paragraphs 47 to 52).

There are three elements in common in these proposals. The first is that, apart from supporting the equitable and sustainable development of developing nations, MDBs must also finance the contribution of these countries to the provision of international public goods – both global and regional – notably the fight against climate change and the prevention of pandemics; the support of biodiversity is absent from these proposals but should certainly be added. The second is the need to have contingency clauses to face the vulnerability of countries associated with climatological and health phenomena and the effects of international crises. These clauses should allow debt service with these institutions to be suspended, and even partly or totally written off under critical conditions. The third is that there is a need to work more closely with the private sector, including to support its contribution to the provision of international public goods.

An essential theme of all these proposals is the need to have concessional credits or donations channeled through the MDBs. These benefits must also favor middle-income countries and create mechanisms that allow partial credit subsidies for the private sector to leverage their investments in the provision of international public goods. To make this possible, it is necessary to significantly increase official development assistance, since it is also essential to expand that received by low-income and vulnerable middle-income countries. Aside from concessional resources, MDB loans should be long term (thirty to fifty years), with more significant grace periods and lower interest rates. To manage the risks associated with exchange rate volatility, they should also lend more in the countries' national currencies, based on the resources they raise with the placement of bonds in those currencies, which would also support the development of capital markets in developing countries.

To ensure concessional credits and donations achieve their full potential, we must consider the terms attached to loans and the policy conditions imposed on recipient countries. These conditions, which can address issues like climate change mitigation, biodiversity conservation, and pandemic preparedness, should be designed with a multi-pronged approach. A recent report by the Climate Policy Initiative advocates for a shift from project-by-project to program-based approaches by MDBs to drive systemic change (CPI, 2023).

The Paris Agreement of 2017 prompted most MDBs to adopt Paris-aligned practices. However, progress on Policy-based operations (PBOs) remains slow. PBOs offer financial support to developing countries in exchange for policy reforms. These reforms typically target areas like public finances, social programs, and key sectors like energy and agriculture. The goal is to strengthen recipient economies and maximize the effectiveness of development investments, ultimately reducing their reliance on aid. As highlighted by the World Resources Institute, MDBs can repurpose their PBO instruments to support climate-resilient development in countries facing debt burdens and climate threats (Neunuebel et al., 2023).

While short-term profit motives often drive private investors, their investments may not always align with long-term sustainability goals. MDBs can provide incentives and de-risk private investment through well-designed policy conditionalities through guarantees or insurance. This ensures that the resulting policies and investments contribute to the broader international public goods agenda. Discussions are ongoing regarding various financial management proposals to expand the relationship between MDB financing and their capital base.

In this regard, there are various financial management proposals to leverage the capital of these institutions and thus allow expanding the ratio between the financing they can provide and their capital base, maintaining in any case the standards that allow these institutions to continue having the best investment grade. In terms of expanding resources, the channeling of the special drawing rights (SDRs) issued by the International Monetary Fund (IMF) through the MDBs, which are already authorized to hold such assets, can contribute to increasing loans from these institutions. In any case, it is necessary to develop a specific instrument that preserves the role of SDRs as reserve assets, based on the experiences of IMF funds that already have such mechanisms (see Section 2).

To fulfill these functions, as well as the more traditional ones, the most important element is the capitalization of the MDBs in the necessary magnitudes. The capitalizations of the World Bank in 2018, as well as those of all institutions after the North Atlantic financial crisis, responded to this demand. However, a complex problem is the doubt about the commitments of major countries to capitalize these institutions today. In fact, in contrast to the North

Atlantic financial crisis, where the G20 asked for the capitalization of all MDBs (G20, 2009), this has been limited in recent years.

The proposals differ significantly in terms of the magnitudes of the financing and capitalizations needed. An independent group of experts of the G20 proposed increasing the annual financing of these institutions to $500 billion[7] by 2030, a third of which would be in official assistance or concessional credits and the rest in nonconcessional credits (G20, 2023a). Given the amount of these institutions' commitments in recent years (excluding the EIB), this means more than doubling the value of their loans. This would require capitalizations but could be supported by the implementation of the recommendations of a previous independent group of experts of the G20 that proposed a new capital adequacy framework for MDBs that would use new standards for risk tolerance, take into account their callable capital and preferred creditor status, and make a broader use of financial innovations that would allow them to share loan risks, among other instruments (G20, 2022).

The magnitude of additional financing proposed by the UN is more ambitious, as it considers the large requirements needed to achieve the SDGs. In fact, the Secretary General's report on this issue highlighted the fact that the relationship between multilateral bank paid-in capital –and, thus, the financing they can provide – and the size of the world economy was significantly reduced in the 1960s and 1970s in the cases of the IBRD and the IDB, as well as other banks in later times (UN, 2023a, Figure 2). For this reason, the UN suggests returning to the 1960 levels, which would require increasing their loans by up to nearly $2 trillion, an amount closer to the financing gap for the SDGs (UN, 2023a, Table 2).

A crucial issue is whether a significant increase in MDBs' lending can be absorbed by developing countries, in particular by those with limited capacity to absorb new debt. This implies that the recapitalization of the banks would need to guarantee the funds for the concessional component of the contribution of these countries to the provision of international public goods, and include new instruments that facilitate private sector investments. They will also require the policies to manage overindebtedness, as discussed in Section 3.

Several of the proposals of the international institution are backed by academic and policy analysts. For example, Gallagher et al. (2023) argue that the main objective of the World Bank, other MDBs, and the IMF should be to guide worldwide capital flows toward growth paths in emerging markets and developing countries that are characterized by being socially inclusive, low carbon and climate resilient. This should be achieved in a way that also ensures fiscal

---

[7] Throughout this Element the sign $ refers to US dollars.

and financial sustainability. On the other hand, Kharas and Battacharya (2023) propose that the IBRD should triple its annual lending to around $100 billion per year with a total loan exposure of $1 trillion by 2030. This must be done, according to their proposals, by working closely with other stakeholders, including the private sector, and using hybrid capital and concessional financing to support both low- and middle-income countries.

It is also crucial that MDBs constitute a comprehensive service network. In the case of the World Bank, this includes its active participation in regional projects, in collaboration with relevant partners, ensuring a wide reach and effective implementation of development initiatives (World Bank, 2023b). Added to this is the need for all MDBs to work with the national development banks (NDBs) and other public institutions in developing countries (Griffith-Jones and Ocampo, 2018). This partnership is essential because public development banks finance between 10 percent and 12 percent of investment worldwide (UN, 2023a) – although there are significant differences in this regard among countries. Strengthening this collaboration would enable NDBs to become effective executors of multilateral programs, thereby enhancing their capacity to serve their local contexts. Furthermore, they could serve as vital channels of information for MDBs, providing insights into their countries' specific financing needs, and ensuring that the support they provide is well aligned with the local priorities and conditions. By fostering such synergies, MDBs and NDBs can collectively drive sustainable development and economic growth in a more coordinated way, thus enhancing their impact.

In relation to climate financing,[8] commitments by MDBs have been growing since the mid-2010s, with a brief interruption in 2019–20 (Figure 2A). In 2022, they more than doubled the levels of financing they had provided in 2015 and have mobilized private finance concurrently. These efforts enabled them to achieve, with significant anticipation, the climate finance levels set for 2025 in the 2019 UN Climate Action Summit (MDBs, 2022). However, their capacity to crowd in private financing for climate change has been quite limited (IMF, 2022, Figure 2.6). Out of the total resources for climate financing, 63 percent was allocated for adaptation, in fact exceeding the 50 percent goal set for developing countries by UNFCCC (2022).

MDBs finance for biodiversity-related activities (both concessional and non-concessional) has been increasing since the mid-2010s but is very limited: only $5.1 billion in 2021. In relative terms, it has represented 2.5 percent of their total financing, with only a few banks contributing significant amounts (OECD, 2023).

---

[8] For a reference to financing to combat pandemics and to support biodiversity, see also Ocampo and González (2024).

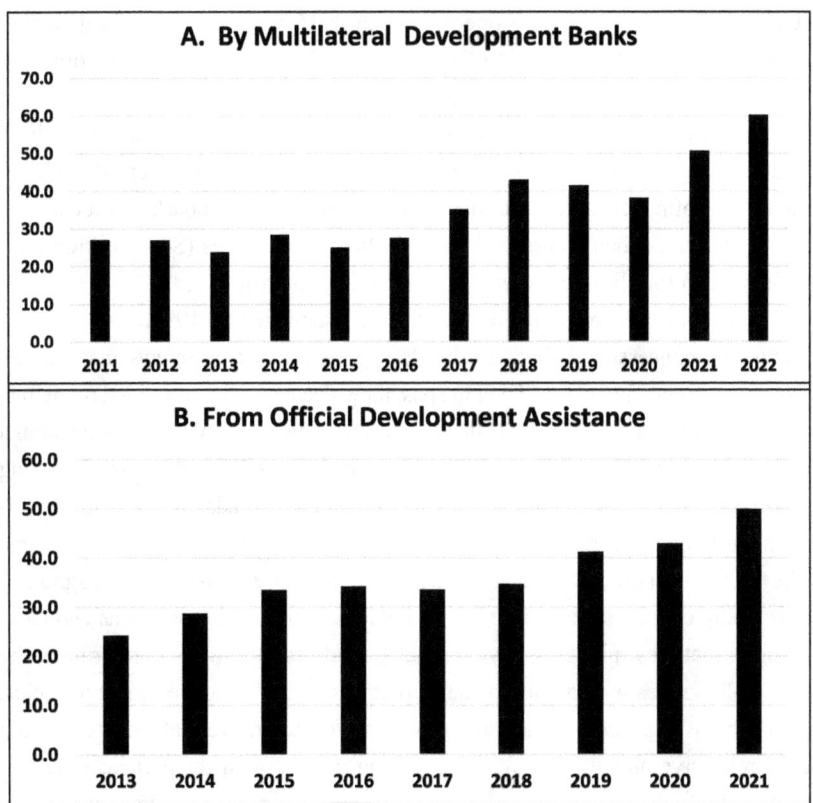

Figure 2 Climate financing (billion dollars). (A) By Multilateral Development Banks. (B) From Official Development Assistance.
Sources: MDBs (2022) and OECD Development Assistance Committee.

The amount of ODA provided for environmental protection[9] has also increased since 2015 (Figure 2B). It has represented about one-fourth of support to African countries but a higher proportion in that is provided to other regions (OECD, 2024). However, in the specific context of climate, studies reveal that countries facing the highest climate vulnerability tend to receive a smaller proportion of climate-specific ODA in relation to their total ODA, with Latin America being a notable case (Development Initiatives, 2023).

In turn, the Green Climate Fund (GCF) operates as a financial mechanism under the United Nations Framework Convention on Climate Change

---

[9] According to the OECD Creditor Reporting System, environmental protection includes environment policy and administrative management, biosphere protection, biodiversity, site preservation, environmental education/training, and environmental research.

(UNFCCC). It became fully operational in 2015 with the aim of supporting developing countries in their efforts toward climate change adaptation and mitigation. The GCF has witnessed significant financial commitments, surpassing $12 billion, since its establishment and mobilized an additional $33 billion. This funding has been invested in climate projects, totaling over $40 billion, including cofinancing in more than 100 countries. As it embarks on its second replenishment, it has committed $12.7 billion in resources ($48.1 billion with cofinancing) for climate projects in developing countries.[10]

The Global Environment Facility (GEF), established in 1991, also provides grants and concessional funds to developing countries for projects that address global environmental issues. Over the past three decades, it has provided more than $25 billion and mobilized $138 billion in cofinancing for more than 5,000 national and regional projects.[11] These projects span various critical areas, including biodiversity conservation, climate change mitigation and adaptation, land degradation, sustainable forest management, and the protection of international waters. The GEF's support has been instrumental in driving environmental progress in developing countries, enabling them to implement innovative solutions and technologies that they might not have been able to afford otherwise. Furthermore, the GEF collaborates with a wide range of partners, including government agencies, civil society organizations, and the private sector, to ensure that the projects are comprehensive and sustainable. By working closely with these stakeholders, it helps to build local capacity and foster long-term environmental stewardship.

At the 2021 Climate COP26 in Glasgow, nations concurred that $100 billion per year for developing countries was necessary for a prolonged climate transition and to fulfill the global emissions target, explicitly including adaptation as a major issue for these countries. This goal replaced the climate finance commitment set in 2009 at the COP15 in Copenhagen, which aimed to mobilize the same amount for developing countries by 2020, a target that was only met in 2022 – that is, two years later than anticipated. This achievement will be primarily attributed to the augmented financing provided by the MDBs (Songwe et al., 2022).

In turn, at the COP27 held in Sharm el-Sheikh in Egypt in 2022, nations reached a consensus to establish a fund for loss and damage, which will offer assistance to countries vulnerable to the impacts of climate change. The specific arrangements for this fund were slated for discussion and consideration at the

---

[10] "Green Climate Fund: New capital to accelerate investments in global climate action," *Press Release*, October 2023, www.greenclimate.fund/news/gcf2-pledging-conference-replenishment.

[11] Global Environment Facility, "New hub supports improved access to climate information," *Press Release*, September 2023, www.thegef.org/newsroom/press-releases/new-hub-supports-improved-access-climate-information.

COP28 meeting in the United Arab Emirates, where it was finally agreed that the mandate focused on addressing loss and damage of developing countries that are more vulnerable to the effects of climate change, responding to their economic and noneconomic consequences.[12]

Finally, there is a final instrument, the global green bonds, which actively involves private agents. In 2022, $487.1 billion of these bonds were issued, slightly lower than the peak of $582.4 reached in 2021, due to the market turmoil. That peak was reached after six years of very fast growth in emissions. The majority came from private sector issuers, accounting for 54 percent in 2022, slightly lower than the previous year's 58 percent. Financial corporations played a significant role, contributing 29 percent of the resources, while nonfinancial corporations contributed 25 percent. European corporates were responsible for nearly half of the private sector's green bond issuance (Climate Bonds Initiative, 2022).

In any case, current climate financing is far below existing estimates of the funds needed, which is between $2.2 trillion and $2.8 trillion annually in emerging markets and developing countries by 2030, according to the International Energy Agency.[13] Furthermore, given the conditions faced by several developing countries in relation to debt (see Section 3), it is unclear whether they can assume further commitments as borrowers, notably given the magnitude of the resources required.

There is also the view in some circles that the fragmentation of the financing mechanisms should be reduced, concentrating the funding in less institutions. The financial architecture for climate is indeed becoming complex and unwieldy. Putting the bulk of resources in less places, with common processes and requirements, would be positive for countries that have to navigate today too many windows. Putting the bulk of this money as capital contribution in MDBs would help multiply financing by the usual leveraging of the balance sheet, as every dollar in capital becomes $4–5 in loans. By contrast, the financing for GCF is one-to-one.

The system of MDBs has been a cornerstone of development finance for decades. Its growing diversity, with new actors like the AIIB and NDB, reflects the evolving development landscape. Looking ahead, MDBs face crucial opportunities. Financing the fight against climate change demands innovative solutions. They can mobilize additional funding and leverage private investment through well-designed policies that incentivize sustainable practices. Similarly, they can bolster economic resilience in developing countries by providing

---

[12] https://unfccc.int/loss-and-damage-fund-joint-interim-secretariat.
[13] www.iea.org/reports/scaling-up-private-finance-for-clean-energy-in-emerging-and-developing-economies/key-findings.

timely support during crises. However, this requires a balance between increased lending and ensuring developing countries' long-term debt sustainability.

Several proposals aim to address these challenges. Increased capitalization, innovative financial instruments, and collaboration with the private sector can all expand lending capacity. Additionally, stronger partnerships with NDBs can improve project implementation. Finally, streamlining the climate finance architecture can enhance efficiency and impact. By seizing these opportunities, MDBs can remain a powerful force for sustainable development. They can mobilize resources, foster innovation, and promote good governance, paving the way for a more prosperous future.

2 The International Monetary System

The current international monetary system is the result of significant changes triggered by the 1971 crisis, when the United States decided to devalue the exchange rate of the dollar vis-à-vis gold. This decision marked a pivotal moment, as the dollar-to-gold standard had been an essential element of the system agreed in 1944 at Bretton Woods. However, by 1971, pressures from trade imbalances and inflation led to the United States unilaterally severing the dollar's link to gold, putting an end to the Bretton Woods system (Eichengreen, 2008; Ocampo, 2017).

The decision of the United States initiated a long period of negotiations among major economies to devise a new framework for the international monetary system. These negotiations were characterized by temporary measures as countries navigated the transition from a fixed exchange rate regime to more flexible exchange rates (Eichengreen, 2011).

The pivotal moment came in 1976, when the basic agreement was ratified at the IMF meetings in Jamaica, known as the Jamaica Accords. These meetings served to amend the IMF articles to legalize this agreement, as well as existing practices. This agreement officially recognized the reality of floating exchange rates, where currency values are determined by market forces rather than being pegged to gold or any other standard (Ocampo, 2017).

The basic elements of this system are the following: (i) There may be multiple reserve currencies, but in practice the fiat dollar has been dominant, followed with a significant margin by the euro and in modest magnitudes by other currencies; (ii) countries can choose the exchange system that they consider most appropriate, which in practice has meant a system of floating rates among the main currencies; (iii) there is a commitment not to "manipulate" the exchange rate, but that concept has not been precisely defined; (iv) countries can continue to regulate capital flows, although they have been liberalized in an important part of the world; and (v) the IMF supervises the countries' macroeconomic policies according to Article IV of the agreement. Added to this, as we will see, is the creation and redesign of credit lines, largely during crises in different parts of the world economy. It is worth adding that, contrary to the visions set in the Bretton Woods agreement, macroeconomic coordination is largely done outside the IMF, through ad hoc groups, initially the OECD-G10, later the G7 and, since the North Atlantic financial crisis, the G20.

An important additional element of the new system was the decision of most European countries to create a regional system, reflecting their preference for stable exchange rates to enhance intra-regional trade. For several developing countries, the transition was not drastic, as they had already been employing other forms of exchange rate flexibility, such as crawling pegs and managed floats (Ocampo, 2017).

Unlike development financing, international monetary reform has not been central to recent global debates. For a long time, the most interesting proposal in terms of reforms is the possibility of using SDRs more actively. This is the reserve currency issued by the IMF itself, which was created in 1969 but has been an instrument with very limited use. According to existing agreements, SDR allocations must be made based on long-term, global needs and to complement the supply of other reserves. There have been four historical allocations: the initial one, in the early 1970s, and those in 1980, 2009, and 2021 – the last two in response to international crises. The 2021 allocation took place after the failure to agree to the issuance in 2020 due to the objection of the United States, although it was ultimately adopted for a sum greater than that initially proposed – the equivalent of $650 billion. Due to the composition of IMF quotas, which is the criterion for allocation to different countries, the bulk of the issuance favored high-income countries (Table 2).

Various analyses on this matter[14] have made interesting proposals. First, they indicate that SDR allocations could be much higher: at least $200 billion a year and even up to $400 billion. It would be advisable, in any case, that they should continue to have a countercyclical nature and be proportional in the long term to the demand for international reserves. For more active use, the main reform that could be adopted is to eliminate the IMF's dual accounting, which currently separates SDRs from the current operations of the Fund. Once this duality is eliminated, the unused SDRs could be considered as deposits of the countries in the IMF, which this entity could therefore use as resources available for its credit operations.

---

[14] Kenen (2010), Ocampo (2017, chapter II), Williamson (2009) and IMF (2011).

Table 2 SDR allocations by level of development (in millions of SDRs)

	Allocations (in million SDRs)				Share in total allocations			
	1970–72	1979–81	2009	2021	1970–72	1979–81	2009	2021
High income: OECD	6,796	7,906	1,08,879	2,80,861	73.6%	65.8%	59.6%	61.5%
United States	2,294	2,606	30,416	79,546	24.8%	21.7%	16.6%	17.4%
Japan	377	514	11,393	29,540	4.1%	4.3%	6.2%	6.5%
Others	4,125	4,786	67,070	1,71,775	44.7%	39.8%	36.7%	37.6%
High income: non-OECD	17	127	3,588	34,958	0.2%	1.1%	2.0%	7.7%
Gulf countries	0	78	2,057	15,251	0.0%	0.7%	1.1%	3.3%
Excluding Gulf countries	17	49	1,531	19,707	0.2%	0.4%	0.8%	4.3%
Middle income	1,488	2,730	54,173	1,32,373	16.1%	22.7%	29.6%	29.0%
China	0	237	6,753	29,217	0.0%	2.0%	3.7%	6.4%
Excluding China	1,488	2,493	47,420	1,03,156	16.1%	20.7%	26.0%	22.6%
Low income	933	1,254	16,095	8,294	10.1%	10.4%	8.8%	1.8%
Total allocations	9,234	12,016	1,82,734	4,56,485	100.0%	100.0%	100.0%	100.0%

Source: Estimates based on IMF data and on World Bank classifications by level of development in 2000. The year 2021 according to the level of development in 2001.

An additional possibility would be that they could be deposited as accounts in IMF Trusts, in MDBs or in multilateral funds to promote certain international objectives. In that regard, two funds have been created by the IMF in recent years: one for balance of payments problems in low-income countries (*Poverty Reduction and Growth Trust*) and another to support prospective longer-term balance of payments stability for low-income and vulnerable middle-income countries, including the management of risks associated with climate change and pandemics (*Resilience and Sustainability Trust*). Both have benefited an increasing group of countries. In both cases it has been necessary to adopt mechanisms that guarantee the liquidity of the SDRs, so that they continue to have the character of a reserve currency.

In turn, in May 2024, the IMF's Executive Board allowed the use of SDRs for the acquisition of hybrid capital instruments issued by prescribed holders (notably MDBs) subject to some constraints to manage liquidity risks. The main objective is to increase the capacity of credit operations of some MDBs for development purposes. The effectiveness of this measure is yet to be assessed, as many IMF members face legal and operational constraints to engage in this type of operations.

There are several other specific proposals aimed at favoring developing countries with the use of SDRs. An important one is to include an additional criterion to the existing quota system used for SDR allocation. This could be based on the countries' per capita income or their demand for international reserves, ensuring that countries with greater needs receive more substantial support. Although this proposal has been on the table for a long time, reaching an agreement on such a criterion has proven to be challenging. Another possibility is that contributions to regional reserve funds could be considered as a criterion for the allocation of SDRs. This would encourage the establishment and strengthening of regional reserve funds, providing a more localized and tailored approach to financial stability. Such funds could act as buffers against regional economic shocks, thereby enhancing the financial resilience in developing countries. This proposal is discussed more extensively in Section 6.

Crisis prevention and management are clearly complementary topics. Preventive actions include prudent macroeconomic management, which is the focus of Article IV consultations, as well as maintaining an appropriate level of international reserves. The accumulation of reserves is required to manage the stronger cyclical shocks developing countries face, but generates significant costs for them. Despite this, there is no mechanism in place to compensate for these costs. Developing countries, therefore, face a disproportionate burden in their efforts to safeguard economic stability. Addressing this imbalance requires innovative financial instruments and international cooperation to ensure that the global financial architecture supports all countries fairly.

The management of shocks from the capital account is a particularly critical issue for developing countries that have access to international private financing, given the procyclical behavior of private capital markets – in terms of both availability and costs (risk margins). For this reason, the possibility of regulating capital flows is an essential issue for these countries, which, in fact, do so more broadly than developed countries. In turn, commodity-dependent economies face the volatility of international prices, which then require specific instruments to manage those fluctuations, a topic to which I will return in Section 5.

In 1997, there was an initiative to establish the convertibility of the capital account as a requirement for IMF members, in addition to the convertibility of current operations that was agreed at Bretton Woods. However, this proposal, which was presented at the institution's annual meeting in Hong Kong, was not adopted. In the opposite direction, after the North Atlantic crisis, the IMF approved the "institutional vision" on capital account management, which points out that liberalization is not always positive and, therefore, that the management of capital flows may be convenient under certain circumstances – although temporarily, according to this vision (IMF, 2012). This decision was adopted after multiple studies that pointed out the risk of capital flow volatility for developing countries, including several by the Fund's technical teams.[15] This institutional vision remains in place.

In terms of the use of IMF financing, there have been significant changes through time. The magnitude of loan disbursement from this institution as a proportion of the world's gross domestic product (GDP) is summarized in Figure 3. Until the 1970s, high-income countries were the most important recipients of the credits of the organization. The situation changed radically in the 1980s, when developing countries became the main claimants. They have continued to be so, except temporarily after the North Atlantic crisis, when some European countries again demanded significant resources from the Fund.

The IMF financing has had a clearly countercyclical behavior. The historical peaks occurred during the Latin American debt and the Asian crises, when they reached the equivalent of 0.3 percent of world GDP in both cases. The maximum amounts reached during the two crises of the twenty-first century – the North Atlantic crisis and the COVID-19 pandemic – led to lower demands: a maximum slightly lower than 0.2 percent of world GDP. However, the peak for high-income countries in the years following the North Atlantic crisis was similar to the

---

[15] See in particular Ostry et al. (2012).

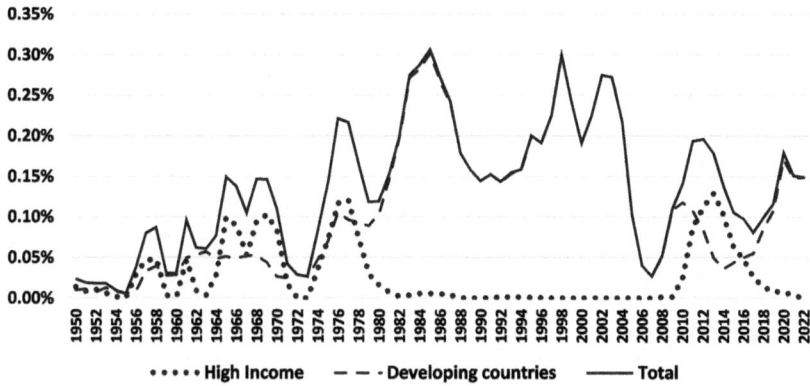

Figure 3 IMF lending relative to world GDP.
Source: Estimated on the basis of IMF data.

historical highs for that group of countries. In contrast, the amounts demanded by developing countries during the COVID-19 pandemic and recent years were much lower than the levels reached during the Latin American debt and Asian crises.

The credit lines have been improving over time. The main recent reforms were adopted in 2009–10, again after the North Atlantic crisis. They included (i) the duplication of all existing lines; (ii) the creation of several contingency lines – the flexible credit and short-term liquidity lines – both without conditionality for countries with strong macroeconomic fundamentals, and the precautionary and liquidity lines, to which a broader group of countries have access, but with conditionality; and (iii) more flexible lines for low-income countries.

The amounts approved under the flexible credit line (FCL) represent a high share of recent IMF program commitments – up to half in some years. Latin American countries have been the ones that have used this line the most: Colombia and Mexico first and Chile and Peru more recently; Colombia is the only one that has made partial disbursements of the approved resources. Their most important element is that they authorize resources that are not necessarily disbursed by countries[16] and, in a sense, represent a type of overdraft facility that gives a positive signal to markets and reduces the need to accumulate international reserves.

In recent times, changes in credit lines have been less important. For low-income countries, interest payments were eliminated in 2015. To face the COVID-19 pandemic, an emergency credit line was approved without conditionality, but for small amounts – up to a country's quota. It was widely used by seventy-nine countries. Although the proposal to approve a swap line was

---

[16] Those that have not been disbursed are not included in Figure 3, which refer to loan disbursements.

unsuccessful, a short-term liquidity line was created but only for 145 percent of the quota, significantly less than the average use of the FCL. Chile was the sole country to use it, but it quickly reverted to using the FCL. In October 2023, the Executive Board implemented improvements in this area, allowing eligible members to concurrently use the flexible and short-term liquidity lines on a prolonged basis for up to 400 percent of their quotas. Additionally, members can access the FCL up to 200 percent of their quotas on a persistent basis, and on a larger scale temporarily but with an ex-ante exit strategy (IMF, 2023b).

In any case, given the financing needs of low- and middle-income countries, significant additional IMF lending is required. According to one estimate, a 127 percent increase in quotas is needed to cover the external crisis finance gap of these countries and 267 percent to cover their short-term gross external financing needs (Mühlich and Zucker-Marques, 2023). These requirements are much higher than the 50 percent quota increase that has been approved. Improvements in the contingency credit lines must be a priority, as they are essential crisis prevention tools and efficient alternatives to reserve accumulation. Another option would be to develop more automatic and unconditional liquidity provision mechanisms that would be available under global shocks and whose objective would be to mitigate contagion, by revisiting, for instance, the Global Shock Window or the Global Shock Activation Mechanism. An interesting complementary proposal recently made by CLAAF (2023) is to create a new IMF instrument of international liquidity provision for emerging and developing economies: an Emerging Market Fund (EMF). This instrument would serve to mitigate the unwarranted effects of systemic liquidity crises on these countries, which are reflected both in the volumes as well as sharp increases in the costs (risk margins) during these crises. The most important feature of the EMF would be its capacity to intervene in a basket of emerging markets bonds during systemic liquidity crises, with the goal of stabilizing those markets. Although a novel proposal for emerging markets, these types of interventions have been widely used by central banks in advanced economies, such as the Federal Reserve and the European Central Bank during times of financial turmoil. The main reason is that, unlike emerging markets, advanced economies have the ability to issue reserve currencies that are widely traded around the world. The EMF seeks to address this fundamental asymmetry between countries that issue reserve currencies and countries that do not. Therefore, it would also help reduce the costs that emerging and developing countries face by the need to accumulate large amounts of foreign exchange reserves to manage the volatility and procyclical pattern of international private capital flows affecting these countries.

In October 2024, there was a decision to reduce the charges, surcharges, and commitment fees affecting the large lending operations of the IMF through the General Resources Account. However, in this regard, the group of developing countries in the Bretton Woods Institutions, the G24, has proposed the suspension of the surcharges for countries with severe balance of payments problems and even a significant permanent reduction in surcharges or their elimination (G24, 2023). These potential reforms aim to provide relief, given the more protracted balance of payments and fiscal needs generated by the higher interest rates that have characterized the world economy in recent years. Given the Fund's balance sheet has strengthened considerably in recent years, the expectation is that considerable support to vulnerable members will be agreed.

The historical behavior of financing to developed versus developing countries is reflected in the evolution of conditionality, which is the most controversial issue of IMF programs. When high-income countries were the main debtors, it was strictly macroeconomic. With the predominance of loans to developing countries, conditionality became more structural, including issues such as privatizations of public sector firms and external trade liberalization. The conditions imposed during the Asian crisis generated strong opposition, which was reflected in a 2002 agreement to return to the principle of macroeconomic conditionality. This principle was expanded in 2009, when it was determined that failure to meet structural goals does not prevent the disbursement of credits. In contrast, in 2018 a modification was approved according to which the IMF can establish conditionality based on governance standards and the fight against corruption, if these factors have macroeconomic impacts. This is a complex criterion because it can lend itself to subjective analysis, even with political elements, and the IMF has no expertise in these areas.

The inclusion of governance is part of a broader set of agreements reached since 2012 that have also included standards on social spending, gender equality, climate change, and digital money. The principle is that they should be considered in surveillance and lending programs to the extent that they have macroeconomic effects – that is, on the balance of payments or on economic and financial stability. According to a recent task force on climate, development and the IMF, the mainstreaming of climate change into IMF activities should deepen, including taking into account in surveillance the macroeconomic implications of financing the climate transition, and finding an appropriate way to analyze the short-term fiscal consolidation versus the long-term resource mobilization needed (TCDIMF, 2023). Whether it should finance climate change through its own funds, including the existing Resilience and Sustainability Trust, is more questionable, as it may be better that such financing be in the hands of funds managed by the MDBs.

In June 2024, the Independent Evaluation Office (IEO) released its analysis on whether the new governance and other standards has implied an excessive expansion of the IMF mandate, to what extent their links with macroeconomic stability are sufficiently clear, and whether the Fund has the means to analyze these issues or should collaborate with other organizations (IMF-IEO, 2024). The evaluation found that the expansion of the scope of the Fund's mandate was in line with its legal framework and the membership's call. However, the implementation of such expansion has not been consistent with the existing resources and expertise. Furthermore, the discussions to broaden the scope of the mandate have lacked a holistic and strategic approach; instead, it has come in the form of a piecemeal and ad hoc set of reforms. The IEO thus recommended that the IMF should prioritize its work in the context of a world economy that has been facing recurrent macroeconomic shocks and is becoming increasingly multipolar, and that the Executive Board should adopt a Statement of Principles to strengthen the collaboration with relevant partners with expertise and comparative advantage in those areas.

The size of the Fund must, of course, continue to reflect the growth and evolving dynamics of the world economy. In this regard, the IMF Board has recommended that member countries increase total quotas by 50 percent. This recommendation aims to ensure that the Fund has sufficient resources to effectively support its member countries in times of economic distress and to maintain global financial stability. In December 2023, the IMF Board of Governors reached an agreement on this quota, underscoring the commitment of the international community to bolster the Fund's capacity. Country authorities were expected to provide their consent for this increase by November 2024, paving the way for the implementation of this critical enhancement of the Fund's resources.

However, the debate on the distribution of quotas to better reflect the relative economic contributions and weights of different economies in the global economy was postponed. The redistribution process is a complex and politically sensitive issue, as it involves adjusting the voting power and financial contributions of member countries based on their current economic standings. This realignment is essential to ensure that emerging economies that have grown significantly over the past few decades have a greater voice and representation in the IMF's decision-making processes. The negotiations for this quota redistribution have been postponed to 2025, allowing more time for member countries to reach a consensus on the new allocation framework. This delay highlights the challenges inherent in balancing the interests of established and emerging economies within the global financial architecture.

The upcoming negotiations will be crucial in addressing these disparities and fostering a more inclusive and equitable IMF governance structure. Successful redistribution will not only enhance the legitimacy and credibility of the institution but also ensure that it remains responsive to the needs of a diverse and dynamic global economy. As such, these discussions are anticipated to be a focal point of international economic diplomacy in the coming years.

A notable difference with the system of MDBs is the weakness of regional institutions in the international monetary system. The largest in relation to regional GDP is the European Stability Mechanism, created in 2012 as a response to the sequence of the North Atlantic and Eurozone crises. It is followed by the Chiang Mai initiative, agreed between the countries of the Association of Southeast Asian Nations (ASEAN), China, Hong Kong, the Republic of Korea, and Japan. It was born in 2000 after the Asian crisis and expanded significantly in 2009, when its currency swap lines were expanded and multilateralized, and were expanded again in 2012. They are followed by the most modest Latin American Reserve Fund, born in 1989 as a successor of the Andean Fund, which had been created in 1978, that now has nine members.

On top of the IMF and regional arrangements, the Bank of International Settlements has been a historical mechanism for short-term financing among its member central banks, and several of these institutions have created swap facilities for their partners. The swap facilities of the US Federal Reserve were particularly important during the North Atlantic and the COVID-19 crises, and to a lesser extent in 2011–12 to support some European countries facing debt crises. The Central Bank of China has also been increasingly active in recent years in the creation of swap facilities.

From this analysis, several recommendations emerge for the reform of the international monetary system. The first is to give the SDRs a much more active role within the system, preferably with a development perspective. The most important reform is, as already indicated, to eliminate the IMF's double accounting and consider unused SDRs as country deposits in the Fund. This can be complemented with deposit of SDRs in the MDBs, or in specific IMF trust funds, to expand the supply of credit to developing countries. Recently, the IMF has approved a mechanism to channel SDRs to MDBs through hybrid capital instruments.

The second recommendation is that the Fund should continue to review and enhance its credit lines, particularly by expanding its contingency facilities, which serve as a crucial instrument for crisis prevention, and that it should reduce or eliminate the surcharges on its lending operations. In the case of the FCL, it is advisable to allow it to be permanent. Additionally, other contingency lines, such as the short-term liquidity line and precautionary and liquidity lines, must be improved to better serve the needs of member countries. In turn, as already pointed out, the Fund could create liquidity mechanisms that would allow interventions to manage adverse cyclical swings in international private capital markets and mitigate contagion. The primary advantage of all the contingency and liquidity facilities is that they will reduce the need for developing countries to accumulate large amounts of international reserves to manage capital account fluctuations and commodity price shocks. As a complement, the institutional vision on capital account regulations must remain in force and even refined to provide more precise guidance and support to member countries navigating complex financial landscapes. This should include the elimination of the view that these regulations should only be temporary.

Third, conditionality must remain strictly macroeconomic and must continue to be subject to rigorous review, as it is still considered the main stigma associated with the Fund's financing. This must include the review of conditionality standards based on governance, anti-corruption measures, and other areas that were adopted over the past decade. Ensuring that these conditions are fair, transparent, and appropriately tailored to the unique circumstances of each member country is essential for maintaining the legitimacy and effectiveness of the Fund's assistance.

Fourth, the increase in Fund quotas that was approved in late 2023 is a significant step forward and must take place as planned; the reforms in the share of member countries' quotas should be reviewed in 2025, as agreed. These reforms should accurately reflect the economic size of different countries in the world economy and increase the voice and participation of developing countries in international economic decision-making. This is a vital institutional issue that will significantly influence the Fund's governance and effectiveness. Ensuring that developing countries have a greater say in the IMF's operations will help address long-standing imbalances and promote a more inclusive and equitable international financial system. This topic will be further elaborated in Section 6.

In addition, and very importantly, expanding the space for regional monetary institutions is essential. The fundamental virtues of these institutions are their members' greater sense of belonging and, therefore, the greater proximity to their demands. An alternative to make them more attractive is to include contributions to these institutions as an additional criterion in the allocation of SDRs.

Finally, there could be greater competition among international reserve currencies. There are proposals to create new international currencies, such as the one that emerged from the BRICS meeting in August 2023, but their viability depends on whether central banks of the member countries support the use of those currencies and, even more, whether they will be accepted by market participants.

3 Sovereign Debt Restructuring

The restructuring of sovereign debt is a relatively empty package of international financial cooperation. Existing mechanisms are often criticized for their inadequacy in addressing the full spectrum of issues faced by debtor countries. The only traditional instrument, established in the mid-1950s, is the Paris Club's restructuring, which covers bilateral official debts with OECD countries. This mechanism, while valuable, is limited in scope and does not address debts owed to non-Paris Club countries, leaving significant gaps in comprehensive debt relief efforts.

During some crises, this framework has been supplemented with ad hoc multilateral mechanisms to address developing countries' pressing sovereign debt issues.[17] A notable example is the Brady Plan launched in 1989, in response to the Latin American crisis of the 1980s. The Brady Plan enabled developing countries, including a significant number from Latin America and from other parts of the world, to restructure their debts. However, this initiative had a major drawback: it arrived too late, almost at the end of the so-called lost decade of Latin America, a period characterized by very slow economic growth and social challenges in the region. Despite its tardiness, the Brady Plan had key virtues, particularly the reduction of debt balances, which alleviated the debt burden of affected countries, and the effective launch of a sovereign bond market. This bond market mechanism has been widely used by developing countries since the last decade of the twentieth century and has become particularly dynamic after the North Atlantic financial crisis.

For low-income countries, another significant debt relief mechanism was the Heavily Indebted Poor Countries Initiative (HIPC) launched in 1996 by the IMF and the World Bank. This initiative aimed to provide comprehensive debt relief to heavily indebted countries and ensure that they did not face unmanageable debt burdens. To take part in the HIPC initiative, countries had to fulfill specific criteria, pledge to implement policies aimed at reducing poverty, and show track record of such efforts. The HIPC was further complemented in 2005 with the Multilateral Debt Relief Initiative, which went a step further by cancelling the debt of eligible countries to the IMF, the World Bank, and the African Development Fund. Additionally, a similar relief mechanism was adopted by the Interamerican Development Bank, benefiting five low-income countries in Latin America and the Caribbean.

---

[17] It can be added that at the beginning of the Second World War the United States launched a debt renegotiation mechanism that benefited the majority of Latin American countries. This mechanism remained in place for several years after the war.

After the 1994 Mexican crisis, there was a discussion on this issue within the framework of OECD's G10. The most important proposal was to introduce new clauses in the bond contracts issued in the United States – collective action clauses (CACs), although they were not called initially that way – a mechanism similar to that which already existed in the London market, where the coordination of creditors in cases of debt restructuring must be managed through a trustee with the prerogative to negotiate or initiate legal procedures.

The only attempt to create a stable institutional framework for debt restructuring took place in 2001–3 at the IMF, as an initiative of the United States. The objective was to create an institutional mechanism to promote agreements between debtors and creditors that would allow unsustainable debts to be restructured through a rapid, orderly, and predictable process while protecting the rights of creditors (Krueger, 2002). The terms of the proposal varied throughout the process, especially with respect to the role of the Fund, due to the opposition of many private actors and civil society to the idea of it playing too active a role in the negotiations or in the approval of the final agreements. On the other hand, it was agreed that domestic public debts should be excluded from these processes. In the final versions of the proposal, although the mechanism would be implemented through an amendment to the Articles of Agreement of the IMF, the body that would be created to guarantee the functioning of the renegotiations would be independent of the IMF Executive Board and its Board of Governors.[18]

The final proposal was rejected by its initial promoter, the United States, under pressure from its financial sector and internal opposition within the Treasury Secretariat, but also from some developing countries (notably Brazil and Mexico) that feared that this mechanism could restrict and make more costly their access to international capital markets, which at that time was already quite limited. The alternative solution, led by Mexico, was the widespread use of CACs in bonds issued in the United States starting in 2003. This experience showed that the costs associated with introducing this clause were minimal. Added to this was the decision by the Eurozone in 2013 to require the inclusion of aggregation clauses in the bond contracts issued by its members, which facilitates the simultaneous renegotiating of multiple bond issues.

Furthermore, following the North Atlantic financial crisis of 2007–9, there were widespread calls for reforms aimed at addressing issues faced by Credit Rating Agencies (CRAs), including their mechanistic way they estimate ratings and their procyclical pattern, which may in fact enhance the probability of debt

---

[18] Hagan (2005) provides an authoritative account of these negotiations, in which he played a central role.

crises, as well as their lack of competitive dynamics, and inherent conflicts of interest. While some reforms were introduced to tackle these concerns, significant challenges persist. The market remains dominated by the three largest CRAs – Moody's, Standard&Poors, and Fitch – collectively controlling over 90 percent of the industry, which limits the competitive pressures necessary to drive change in their practices. Unlike other financial institutions, these agencies operate without formal regulation and oversight. Moreover, their reliance on CRA ratings continues to be driven by structural conflicts of interest and conflicting regulatory and investment mandates. However, the COVID-19 pandemic, ongoing technological advancements, mounting systemic risks, and the increasing complexity of global finance underscore the critical need to fundamentally reassess the entire informational framework supporting sovereign borrowing (United Nations, 2022).

For its part, Argentina's defeat in its 2013–14 litigation in US courts led to new solutions. The specific problem was the particular interpretation of the "pari passu clause," which forced that country to make full payment of the debt with the creditors who had not participated in the two renegotiations that the country had carried out in previous years – the so-called dissident creditors or holdouts. The solution was to make bond issues that included both the revision of that clause[19] and the aggregation mechanisms that Europeans had developed. Mexico led the way again in November 2014, when it inserted the new clauses in a New York bond issue – Kazakhstan had done the same in a new London issue during the previous month – without affecting the cost of the debt. It also replaced the fiscal agent with a trustee to represent the bondholders in negotiations with the debtors – a system similar to that of London.

In any case, aggregation does not exclude the possibility of blocking majorities in individual issues and does not guarantee coherence between bond contracts and other debt contracts, such as loans from banking consortia. To these considerations, we can add the caveat that, even if the revised CACs could solve future problems, they do not resolve the legacy of existing debt for some time and may even worsen it until aggregation clauses are included in all the debt contracts.

Recent problems in this field are associated with the COVID-19 pandemic and the complexities that the global economy has faced subsequently, including its slow recovery and the high interest rates generated when global inflation accelerated after the Russian invasion of Ukraine in February 2022.

---

[19] This clause generally means "of equal rank," but the New York courts interpreted it in the Argentine case as "equal pro rata payments," a reading that gave the holdouts greater bargaining power. A change was introduced in the new contracts that eliminates any possibility of interpreting the clause as pro rata.

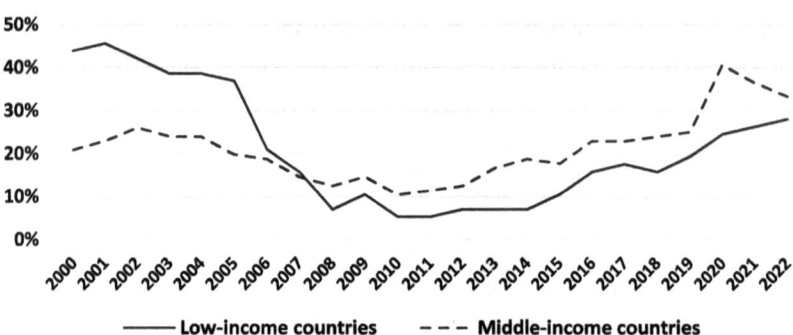

Figure 4 Proportion of developing countries with high debt levels (over 70 percent of GDP).
Source: Estimates based on World Bank data.

Figure 4 shows the proportion of developing countries with high levels of public debt – defined as debts that exceed 70 percent of GDP – as assessed by the IMF and the World Bank. The share of high-indebted low-income earners, which had fallen significantly with the 2005 multilateral debt relief policy, began to rise again since the mid-2010s and now reaches almost 30 percent. In turn, the proportion of middle-income countries with high debt decreased in the first decade of the twenty-first century, but began to increase in the second decade, reaching a new peak in 2020 and still remains above the levels of the previous two decades.

Due to the high levels of interest rates that have recently characterized the global economy and the high-risk spreads in global private financial markets, even countries that do not face high levels of debt may be characterized as facing debt distress. This is also reflected in the high level of interest payments as a proportion of public sector revenues, as well as in the fact that new issues that, in a sense, replace old debt would have higher levels of interest payments. Figure 5 indicates that, on a broader definition, more than half of low-income countries – that is, those with access to IDA – face high debt risks, and another third of them face moderate risk, again according to the analysis of the Bretton Woods institutions.[20] It should be added that, according to IMF projections, all groups of developing countries have and will continue to have in the coming years higher debt levels than those of 2019 (IMF, 2023a, Graph 3.1).

---

[20] In turn, the *Economist* magazine also identified, in mid-2022, fifty-three vulnerable countries, which have defaulted on their debt payments or are at high risk of suffering difficulties due to them. They are mostly low-income countries, but there are also some middle-income ones. As a group, they represent 18% of the world's population and 5% of global GDP. See www.economist.com/finance-and-economics/2022/07/20/the-53-fragile-emerging-economies, July 20, 2022.

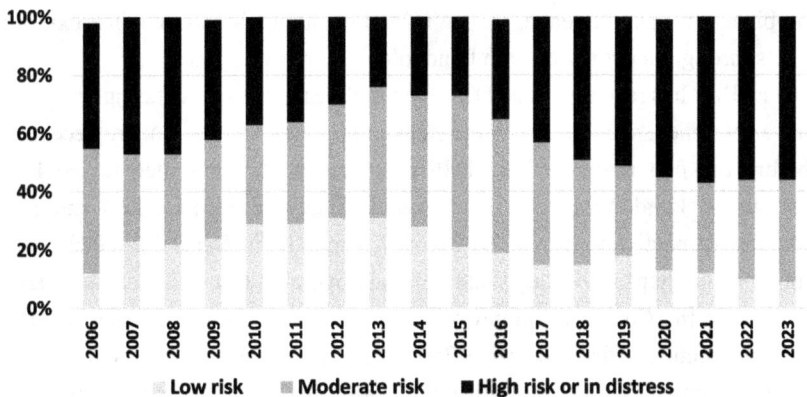

Figure 5 Risk of debt distress among IDA-eligible countries.
Source: Joint World Bank–IMF debt sustainability framework for low-income countres (LIC DSF) database.

During the pandemic, the G20 and the Paris Club launched the Debt Service Suspension Initiative (DSSI) for low-income countries. With support from the World Bank and the IMF, the ISSD helped withhold payments for $12.9 billion from forty-eight countries, among the seventy-three eligible between May 2020 and December 2021 (World Bank, 2022a). However, it was only a temporary and partial solution, and it did not reduce debt levels and achieved minimal participation from private creditors. Since its expiration, it is estimated that almost half of the eligible countries are at risk of difficulties repaying their debts.

At the end of 2020, the G20 and the Paris Club also launched, for DSSI-eligible countries, the Common Framework for Debt Treatment. It aims to improve the coordination of debt treatments and incorporate the participation of a broad base of creditors, including new official creditors – China, India, and Saudi Arabia, among others – to guarantee comparable burden sharing. For countries where debt is unsustainable, the program can offer a reduction in its net present value to regain sustainability. When debt is sustainable, but the country faces liquidity issues or high debt costs, it can offer rescheduling or reprofiling of debt.

However, this mechanism has not been able to speed up debt restructurings. Only four countries have requested to take part in the Common Framework so far: Chad, Ethiopia, Ghana, and Zambia. The United Nations, among other organizations and analysts, has proposed using an improved version of this mechanism, as noted in this section below. Several middle-income countries need immediate debt relief but do not meet DSSI requirements. Some, such as Lebanon, Sri Lanka, and Suriname, have already defaulted on their payments and others, such as Egypt, Pakistan, and Tunisia, are facing serious debt problems. In Latin America, Argentina and Ecuador restructured their external debts through negotiations with bondholders in recent years.

The IMF has recently argued that the timelines in the restructuring processes have shortened, specifically on the steps in the restructuring that are necessary before the first review of the IMF program can be presented to the IMF Executive Board. While this process took Chad and Zambia, 12.4 and 10.4 months, respectively, it took Sri Lanka 8.8 months in December 2023 and 8 months for Ghana in January 2024 (Global Sovereign Debt Roundtable, 2024).

Outside the Common Framework, Argentina and Suriname made separate debt restructuring deals with the Paris Club and its private creditors in 2022 (World Bank, 2023a), and Sri Lanka with its official creditors in 2024. Argentina's agreement involved restructuring $2 billion in arrears from a 2014 deal over six years at a reduced interest rate. Suriname's deal restructured $58 million in arrears and debt service payments due in 2023–4 over an extended seventeen-to-twenty-year period, with a possible further restructuring in 2025 based on the IMF program outcome. Additionally, Suriname renegotiated $600 million of its dollar-denominated bonds in 2022 into a new ten-year amortizing bond. Sri Lanka's economic crisis led to defaulting on debts to both official and private creditors, prompting talks with China, India, and bondholders. In July 2023, Sri Lanka approved a plan to convert Treasury bills into longer-maturity Treasury bonds as part of its domestic debt restructuring strategy. In July 2024, it reached an agreement with its bilateral creditors, including China and India.

Furthermore, challenges persist regarding debt transparency for both borrowers and creditors. Borrowers often face issues due to governance gaps, weak legal frameworks, limited institutional capacity, and inefficient reporting systems, which can lead to inaccuracies in recording and reporting debt positions, thereby reducing accountability. While creditors generally maintain sound lending practices, there is room for improvement in information sharing and transparency. Making information more accessible can promote a more responsible lending environment. These transparency issues are particularly acute in developing countries, where factors such as resource constraints, weak information systems, and inadequate coordination among government agencies hinder effective debt management, reporting, and accountability. This lack of transparency can encourage authorities to bypass fiscal rules or accept unfavorable borrowing terms, undermining sustainable development (IMF, 2023a). Addressing these challenges through enhanced governance, improved information sharing, and capacity building efforts is crucial to encourage responsible borrowing practices, support robust economic policymaking, and ultimately foster sustainable growth for borrowing nations (Ocampo and González, 2024).

The absence of consistent, comprehensive, and promptly updated public debt information presents significant obstacles within the international debt framework. Specifically, discrepancies or inaccuracies in debt records from various sources can hinder efficient debt management, compromise the accuracy of debt sustainability assessments, and delay timely and fair debt restructuring initiatives (Rivetti, 2022). The COVID-19 crisis and its aftermath have emphasized the pressing need to enhance debt transparency, underscoring the urgency for debt settlement and restructuring efforts.

Ambitious reforms are therefore needed. In September 2020, the IMF highlighted the need to improve the contractual approach to debt restructuring (IMF, 2020). At the same time, it emphasized the growing problems associated with collateralized debt that is not in the form of bonds and the lack of transparency in that area. But these contractual agreements are also insufficient, because half of the sovereign bonds of emerging and developing countries lack expanded collective action clauses that allow the simultaneous renegotiation of several debt contracts.

For all these reasons, designing a permanent institutional mechanism to restructure sovereign debts is essential (United Nations, 2023a and 2023b). This statutory approach, as it has been called in the debates, should create an institution that should preferably operate in the United Nations, but could also do so in the IMF, as was attempted at the beginning of the century, if decisions are made by a specialized agency independent of the Fund's Executive Board and Board of Governors. The corresponding body should serve as a framework for renegotiation in three stages, each with fixed deadlines: voluntary renegotiation, mediation, and arbitration.

Even if these negotiations begin, it will be a long and complex process. For this reason, an essential complement is an ad hoc mechanism, which could be, as already noted, the expansion of the Common Framework for Debt Restructuring, as the United Nations (2023a and 2003b) and other institutions have suggested. To achieve this, it would be essential that this scheme meet the following six essential criteria:

- Include a clear and shorter time frame.
- Suspend debt payments during negotiations – that is, operate temporarily as a standstill mechanism.
- Include the necessary mechanisms to guarantee debt sustainability, including debt reductions – "haircuts," as they are called in the debate – and not only lower interest rates and extended maturities.

- Establish clear processes and precise rules to guarantee that all debts are renegotiated, and all creditor countries and private creditors participate – a topic on which I return below in this section.
- Priority rules that favor lenders who have provided financing during the crisis.
- Expand eligibility to middle-income countries.

One possibility is that the ad hoc mechanism, whether a common framework or another that is adopted, is supported by the MDBs, either the World Bank or regional banks (Ocampo, 2022). These institutions would serve as a structured renegotiation platform, with all creditors expected to participate again. The advantage of this mechanism lies in the fact that the bank could facilitate financing, which would help address the macroeconomic challenges faced by overindebted countries but also provide these countries resources to partially pay their debts, thus providing an incentive for creditors to participate. The process should again include all debts, and payments made during the renegotiations subject to rigorous oversight by the MDB in charge of the process. If the result is the issuance of a new bond, as in the Brady Plan, it would be advisable to establish a guarantee for those who continue to be in possession of those bonds, which would also contribute to a successful restructuring.

As the previous proposals indicate, it should be emphasized that the traditional separation between official and private creditors has become more complex with the advent of new official lenders that do not belong to the Paris Club – notably China. As shown in Figure 6, private creditors now hold the majority of public and publicly guaranteed debt in low-income countries, according to IMF data. Additionally, new forms of borrowing and credit guarantees with diverse creditors have further complicated this landscape. This may imply that future "aggregations" refer not only to liabilities with private creditors but to *all* obligations, including multilateral and official credits. For this reason, a global debt registry is necessary, which should include all types of debt with the private sector, as well as with different public entities and governments. This mechanism is also essential to give transparency to any debt restructuring mechanism.

A complex problem is whether debts to the MDBs should be included in the restructuring processes, as was done in 2005 for low-income countries. This is the proposal of a recent work by well-known analysts in this field (Zucker-Marques, Volz, and Gallagher, 2023). The main virtue of this proposal is that a significant proportion of the debts of highly indebted low-income countries is with the MDBs. This problem is particularly important for Sub-Saharan African countries. To achieve this purpose, it would be essential to guarantee the flow of development aid to cover the associated losses in which these banks would be essential.

Financing for Development 33

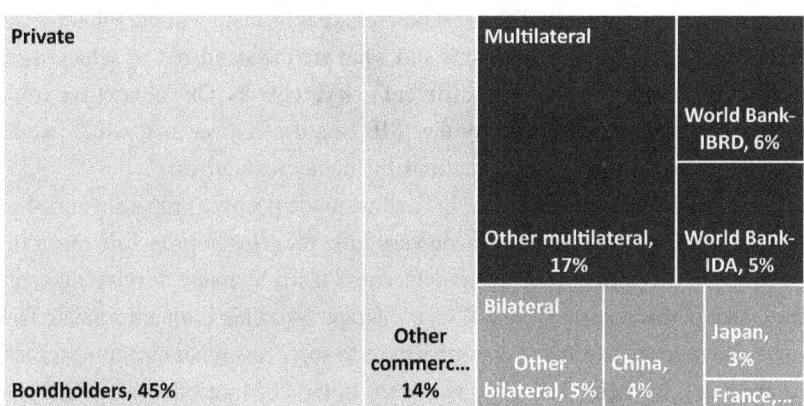

Figure 6 Public and publicly guaranteed debt, by creditor and creditor type in LMICS.
Source: World Bank (2023a).

To reduce the risk of future debt crises, the World Bank (2022b) and other analysts suggest a broad adoption of debt instruments like state-contingent bonds, offering variable returns linked to economic conditions or commodity prices. These instruments would help alleviate the pressure on sovereign balance sheets during economic downturns and hold potential advantages for investors. It is also essential to develop domestic bond markets to reduce the exchange rate risk that countries face – though developing those markets is a long process. At the domestic level, it should be added that avoiding future crises also requires developing countries to adopt sustainable fiscal frameworks and countercyclical macroeconomic policies that should include the use of commodity funds for countries that have an export dependence on agricultural or mining products.

Given the large needs associated with financing mitigation and adaptation to climate change, as well as the biodiversity issues faced by many developing countries, debt renegotiations should also include the very active use of debt-for-nature swaps. A great example is that of Ecuador, which in May 2023 signed the largest debt-for-nature swap deal, which implied convert $1,628 billion of debt into commitments to the conservation of the Galapagos islands. Another good example is the debt-for-nature swap between Belize and the Nature Conservancy in 2022, in which a $553 million debt was restructured, with $364 million being exchanged for a "blue loan" from Credit Suisse to fund marine conservation efforts. A third one is Cabo Verde, who entered into a debt-for-nature swap with Portugal that would initially cover €12 million of debt repayments scheduled until 2025, but if shown to be effective, it would be extended to all the €140 of debt.

An additional element in the agenda must be to design regulation standards for credit-rating agencies. They should include information about what factors are included in the risk evaluations and what are the standards by which these institutions classify countries in different risk categories. One alternative could be global standards approved by the IMF Board of Governors, which would then be adopted as national regulations by member countries.

Finally, it should be noted that, in contrast to the positive proposals regarding MDBs, the 2023 G20 Summit made very little progress in proposals regarding solutions to the problems of overindebtedness faced by many developing countries (see, in this regard, G20, 2023c, Paragraph 54). This is an unfortunate fact, given the urgency that many countries have to solve this fundamental restriction on their development. The issue was back in the 2024 agenda of the G20 and should be in that of the fourth UN Conference on Financing for Development.

In conclusion, the landscape of sovereign debt restructuring reveals a complex tapestry of historical mechanisms and ongoing challenges. Despite the long-standing Paris Club framework established in the mid-1950s, which addresses bilateral official debts with OECD countries, its limitations are evident in the gaps it leaves concerning non-Paris Club creditors. Ad hoc multilateral efforts like the Brady Plan of 1989 provided significant relief post-Latin American crisis, yet its delayed implementation underscored missed opportunities during the region's tumultuous "lost decade." Meanwhile, initiatives such as the HIPC and subsequent Multilateral Debt Relief Initiative sought to alleviate debt burdens for low-income nations, albeit with varying success and coverage. The introduction of CACs and other contractual innovations aimed to enhance debt restructuring mechanisms has been an advance, but challenges persist in achieving comprehensive creditor participation and ensuring sustainability. Recent discussions have further highlighted the urgency of reforming the international debt framework, emphasizing the need for enhanced transparency, inclusive debt relief mechanisms, and sustainable borrowing practices. As discussions continue within global forums and institutions, the quest for a stable and equitable sovereign debt restructuring mechanism remains imperative to address the evolving complexities of global finance and support sustainable development across countries.

4 International Tax Cooperation

The freedom of capital movement by multinational corporations (MNCs), and by financial firms and asset owners has been an increasingly relevant feature of the global economy. The free movement of capital and the opportunities for the geographical dispersion of firms create, however, fundamental challenges for tax authorities. Different national taxation norms and interstices between tax administrations create conflicts of interest among all actors, and double taxation arising from the concurrent exercise by two or more countries of their taxation rights may have an adverse effect on investments. On the other hand, lack of administrative coordination between tax jurisdictions facilitates capital flight and loss of vital tax revenue, in particular due to profit shifting by multinationals and tax avoidance/evasion by individuals.

A large network of bilateral tax treaties has historically managed international tax cooperation. These treaties follow two basic models, designed by the OECD and the UN, which are generally viewed as favoring the countries where the headquarters of MNCs are located and the nations where they have investments, respectively.

In recent decades, the tax reforms adopted by developed countries and the OECD's soft-law standards has created a landscape where MNCs take advantage of tax benefits, preferential regimes, and tax havens to reduce their worldwide payments. This situation became evident with the North Atlantic financial crisis, which prompted the G20 to commission the OECD to study the causes and potential solutions to the low taxation levels of international firms. As a result of this, the Base Erosion and Profit Shifting (BEPS) negotiations were launched in 2013, resulting in a report in 2015 and a multilateral convention signed in 2016 (OECD, 2016), so far ratified by sixty-five countries.[21] It was followed by the OECD Inclusive Framework, now encompassing more than 140 countries. The OECD Global Forum on Transparency and Exchange of Information for Tax Purposes, launched in 2000, opened up to non-OECD countries in 2009, and now includes 171 jurisdictions.[22]

There is also the Committee of Experts on International Cooperation in Tax Matters, a subsidiary body of the UN Economic and Social Council, which became a regular committee in 2004 – after a long period as an ad hoc body – and was upgraded in the UN Conference on Financing for Development in 2015. Its main mandate is to help prevent double taxation and nontaxation and to assist countries to broaden their tax base, strengthen tax administration, and curb international tax evasion and avoidance, supporting in particular developing countries. It is also in charge of updating the UN model for bilateral tax treaties, its traditional task.

A major problem of the global tax system is that, indeed, the persistently large amount of profits is shifted to tax havens: $1 trillion in 2022. This is the equivalent of 35 percent of all the profits made by multinational companies

---

[21] www.oecd.org/tax/treaties/beps-mli-signatories-and-parties.pdf.
[22] www.oecd.org/tax/transparency/who-we-are/members/.

outside of their headquarter country. According to the analysis by the EU Tax Observatory (2024), information exchange has been effective in reducing untaxed offshore financial wealth. However, despite this advance, the global tax revenues loss due to profit shifting of profits from MNCs to tax havens continue to be high –close to 10 percent (see Figure 7) – and the effective tax rates for billionaires very low – between 0 percent and 0.5 percent of their wealth, according to their estimates. One of the main reasons for this is the lack of a global registry of beneficial owners, not just for financial assets but also for nonfinancial assets and luxury assets such as yachts, private jets, real estate, art, and other property accessible particularly to the wealthy of the world.

The outcome of the OECD Inclusive Framework negotiations was the October 2021 agreement, aimed at curbing the negative consequences of the digitalization of the economy and the so-called race to the bottom. It comprised two elements. Under Pillar I, a small share of the global profits of MNCs would be allocated to the countries where their customers are located, based on the countries' share of worldwide sales, even if they sell remotely. However, it only applies to very large and profitable firms – those with annual global turnover exceeding €20 billion and profit margins of at least 10 percent of revenue – and only for 25 percent of their "residual" profit, defined as that exceeding a 10 percent profit margin. In turn, Pillar II established a minimum effective tax rate of 15 percent for multinationals with a turnover exceeding €750 million.

Although the agreement represented progress in tax cooperation, it has faced several criticisms. On Pillar I, developing countries consistently advocated for a meaningful reallocation of taxing rights to source countries – that is, where these companies conduct their activities. The African Tax Administration

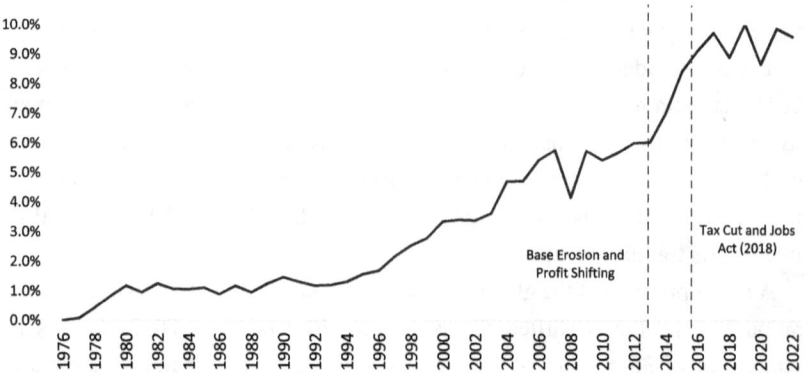

Figure 7 Corporate tax revenue loss due to profit shifting (percent of global corporate tax collection).

Source: Wier and Zucman (2023), and EU Tax Observatory (2024).

Forum (ATAF) demanded that a percentage of all global profits of multinationals, whether routine or residual, should be apportioned to the countries where these companies do business.

In turn, during the negotiations, the group of developing countries in the Bretton Woods Institutions, the G24, put forward a proposal with four basic elements (G24, 2019 and 2020):

- The removal of the physical presence and its replacement with the Significant Economic Presence as the rule for taxation at the source.
- A formulaic approach to determine the taxable profits of the multinational, called fractional apportionment – a system widely used by federal countries for the national taxation systems. Fractional apportionment, like unitary taxation, would allocate a portion of the global profits of the enterprise to different jurisdictions where it has a significant economic presence based on a formula that contemplates some simple, objective criteria, giving balanced recognition to both supply and demand factors that contribute to profit creation (sales, assets, and employees).
- That source countries should have a priority in applying the minimum tax, including on MNCs' interest earnings, royalties, service payments, and capital gains.
- And administrative simplicity, which fractional apportionment will address.

Unfortunately, these proposals were not accepted.

In turn, the tax rate adopted under Pillar II has been deemed as too low by many analysts, and it is below the 21 percent proposed by the United States and well below the current corporate tax rates of African and Latin American countries (around 25 percent). Although it was intended as an effective rate, several carveouts imply that it will be below 15 percent.

Another problem of this two-pillar agreement is that signatories are required to remove unilateral measures like digital services taxes, a condition that is unsatisfactory for many developing economies as it would limit their ability to tax digital MNCs in the future. Additionally, although mandatory dispute resolution was ultimately included in Pillar I, developing countries continue to oppose a wider scope to include transfer pricing disputes. Despite all these weaknesses, most OECD Inclusive Framework members accepted the agreement – the exceptions were Nigeria, Kenya, Pakistan, and Sri Lanka. In any case, Pillar I still needs a Convention to be effective, and its approval by all parliaments, particularly by US Congress. This is an additional uncertainty. A current draft text is being negotiated, but reservations remain from three countries – Brazil, India, and Colombia.

According to all estimates, the greatest benefits of these tax reforms are expected to go to high-income countries, where the headquarters of the main multinationals are located (EU Tax Observatory, 2024). In response to the marginal benefits for the developing world, African countries proposed negotiating a UN tax convention. After the approval of a General Assembly resolution in December 2022,[23] it became the central issue in international tax debates in 2023. Based on the three alternatives proposed by the UN Secretariat (UN, 2023c), on November 2023 the UN approved, by a wide margin,[24] the establishment of an intergovernmental committee to draft the terms of reference for a UN Framework Convention on International Tax Cooperation aiming at an effective and inclusive international tax cooperation system.

The Independent Commission for the Reform of International Corporate Taxation has presented proposals that could be considered in these negotiations (ICRICT, 2022a and 2022b). They include the adoption of a global formulaic approach for MNCs, according to which they would have a global income tax return and pay taxes in the countries where they operate based on production, sales, and employment. They also include a stronger minimum corporate tax rate – the group proposed an effective tax rate of 25 percent with no carveouts during the OECD negotiations – as well as the global asset registry and the possibility of adopting wealth taxes at the global level.

In turn, there is a growing recognition that today's tax systems tend to be sharply regressive at the top of the distribution, with high net worth individuals who tend to pay proportionally less in taxes than other socioeconomic groups. To face this issue, the EU Tax Observatory (2024) has proposed a global tax for billionaires (somewhat less than 3,000 globally) equivalent annually to 2 percent of their wealth. Based on this recommendation, the Brazilian G20 presidency proposed the creation of a coordinated global minimum tax on the superrich following this proposal.[25] This innovative global framework could generate an annual revenue of $250 billion, also promoting income redistribution and reducing wealth concentration.

As a result of the work of the ad hoc Intergovernmental Committee that met in 2024, the Chair's Proposal for the Terms of Reference of the UN Convention was approved in August 2024 (United Nations, 2024c). According to this Proposal, the objectives of the Convention should be to establish a fully inclusive and effective system of tax cooperation and an appropriate system of

---

[23] UN General Assembly Resolution 77/2044 of December 30, 2022.
[24] In all, 125 votes in favor, 48 against, and 9 abstentions.
[25] See in this regard the proposals presented by Zucman (2024) to Brazil as president of the 2024 G20 Summit.

governance in this area of international collaboration. To guarantee this, some of the guiding principles of the Convention should be the following:

- "be universal in approach and scope and should fully take into account the different needs, priorities, and capacities of all countries, including developing countries, in particular countries in special situations; (...)
- take a holistic, sustainable development perspective that covers in a balanced and integrated manner economic, social and environmental policy aspects;
- be sufficiently flexible, resilient and agile to ensure equitable and effective results as societies, technologies and business models and the international tax cooperation landscapes evolve; (...)
- provide for rules that are as simple and easy to administer as the subject matter allows; (...)
- require transparency and accountability of all taxpayers" (United Nations, 2024c, paragraph 9).

Based on these principles, the Proposal indicates that the Convention should include commitments in several areas: "fair allocation of taxing rights, including equitable taxation of multinational enterprises; addressing tax evasion and avoidance by high net-worth individuals (...); effective mutual administrative assistance in tax matters, including with respect to transparency and exchange of information for tax purposes; addressing tax-related illicit financial flows, tax avoidance, tax evasion and harmful tax practices; and effective prevention and resolution of tax disputes" (United Nations, 2024c, paragraph 10). However, these suggested commitments are only formulated in general terms. To achieve some of these commitments, it proposes two early protocols: one on taxation of income derived from the provision of cross-border services, and a second to be chosen from a list of priority areas that includes taxation of the digitalized economy, measures against tax-related illicit financial flows, and tax evasion and avoidance by high net worth individuals, among other issues (United Nations, 2024c, paragraphs 15 and 16). Finally, although, as already indicated, it also proposes that the Convention should establish a system of governance for international tax cooperation, it does not suggest any specific proposal in this area.

Based on these principles and commitments, the future UN convention and the principles it establishes should thus encompass work in the following areas:[26]

- Taxation of multinationals' profits, including but not limited to a fair reallocation of taxing rights between countries, underpinned by the principle of unitary taxation and formulary apportionment of all large multinationals' profits across different jurisdictions. This would require the development of

---

[26] See in particular the proposals by ICRICT (2024a and 2024b).

a nexus rule based on the principle of significant economic presence, whereby a taxable presence will be created in the country when a nonresident enterprise has significant business activities.
- Coordinated taxation of windfall or excess profits. The strengthening of anti-avoidance instruments such as a 25 percent global effective minimum tax on the profits of multinational corporations.
- The development of coordinated mechanisms for digital services taxes.
- Clear criteria for taxing activities associated with the exploitation of natural resources.
- Public country-by-country reporting of multinationals' economic activities based on the robust Global Reporting Initiative standard for public reporting on tax.[27]
- Common principles and minimum standards for the taxation of the income and the wealth (both flows and stocks) of the world's superrich and each country's very rich individuals, including anti-avoidance instruments such as a global minimum tax on their income, and a commitment by all countries to ensure effective taxation of wealth as a complement to taxation of income. Indeed, the proposal of a minimum tax on the very rich and superrich could also be negotiated as one of the early protocols of the Convention, hopefully after an agreement in the G20 negotiations.
- Common principles and minimum standards for ensuring transparency of wealth ownership, including through the creation of a global asset register that identifies final beneficial owners of all assets, combining public data components, and components held privately for tax authorities and other enforcement bodies.

The challenges of the negotiations must not be underestimated. Most developed countries voted against the agreement and have refused so far to provide the necessary funding to ensure that all member states – particularly poorer and smaller developing countries – are able to effectively participate in the negotiations. A positive sign was that the Chair's Proposal for the Convention had much fewer negative votes than the November 2023 General Assembly resolution,[28] and in particular most European countries abstained rather than voted against. The hope is that all developed countries will realize that it is in their own best interests to join and support this inclusive process.

There are two additional issues in international tax cooperation that must be addressed. The first relates to the system of governance for international tax cooperation. One of the alternatives is the transformation of the UN Committee

---

[27] See in this regard GRI (2021).
[28] In all, 110 votes in favor, 44 abstentions, and only 8 against.

of Experts on International Cooperation in Tax Matters into an intergovernmental organ. This proposal has been defeated twice: in 2004, when the Committee was given a permanent character; and in 2015, when the Group of 77 presented a similar proposal at the Addis Ababa Financing for Development Summit. The alternative that some countries have suggested is to create a new UN organization to support international tax cooperation.

The second is the weakness of regional tax cooperation processes. In this regard, the OECD has its own cooperation system for its members, which has been in place for a long time. The African Tax Administration Forum is also one of those mechanisms. In turn, the Latin American and Caribbean Taxation Platform (PTLAC) was created in July 2023 under the leadership of Brazil, Chile, and Colombia. Both the African and the Latin American mechanisms must expand tax cooperation activities among its members, so that we may build a fair, inclusive, and sustainable international tax system from the bottom-up.

As the growing mobility of capital across national borders poses serious problems for national fiscal authorities committed to taxing income from multinationals, rich individuals, and the wealthy, the pressure for effective international cooperation is increasing. The ongoing negotiations of a UN Convention and the proposal that the G20 should promote taxing the superrich are major opportunities in this regard. Strengthening international collaboration could increase the fiscal resources available to countries, and this would bring further benefits, including disincentives to capital flight, increased fiscal and macroeconomic stability, and greater resources available for poverty and inequality reduction, investment in infrastructure, public utilities, and in climate mitigation and adaptation.

5 International Trade

International trade has experienced two adverse trends in recent decades. The first is the significant slowdown in growth since the North Atlantic financial crisis. As Figure 8 indicates, world trade experienced a new boom between the mid-1980s and 2007, similar to that which had taken place after the Second World War until the mid-1970s, and in both cases faster than world GDP growth. In fact, the export growth rate more than doubled that of world GDP growth in 1986–2007 – marking the highest "elasticity" in history, to use the economics terminology (see Figure 8).

The recent trends are even more adverse. The growth of world trade since the North Atlantic crisis has been the slowest in the post-Second World War period (see Figure 8 again). According to the "World Trade Monitor" of the Netherlands

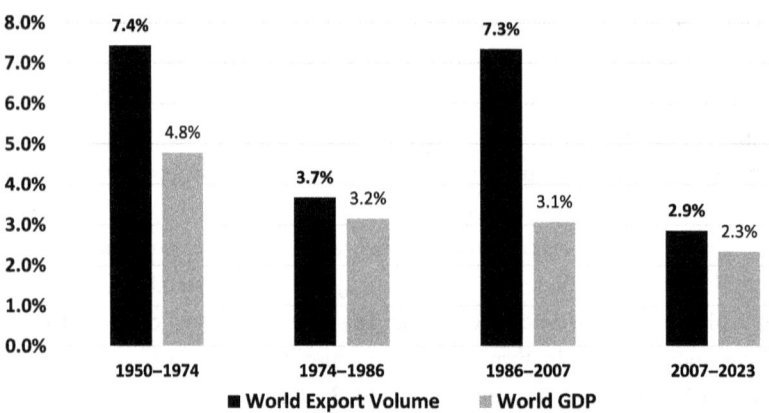

Figure 8 Annual growth of world exports and GDP.
Source: United Nations until 2007, IMF since then. GDP is estimated at market prices.

Bureau for Economic Public Analysis, world exports experienced a sluggish growth rate in 2021–3, 1.1 percent in volume terms. Although there was an uptick in value terms in 2022, driven by the surge in commodity prices generated by the invasion of Ukraine, exports declined again in 2023.[29]

There are two additional unfavorable trends. The most important is the proliferation of trade interventions that have taken place in recent years, which have generated a significant number of concerns raised in the meetings of the WTO Council for Trade in Goods and a significant increase in the countervailing duties (WTO, 2023). According to the IMF's New Industrial Policy Observatory (NIPO) data, interventions affecting international trade have been more frequent in advanced than in emerging and developing economies, particularly in North America, Europe, and Central Asia, followed by East Asia (China in particular). The most frequent interventions are domestic subsidies and import barriers, followed by export barriers and subsidies (see Table 3 and the broader analysis by Evenett et al., 2024).

The additional negative trend is the effects of geopolitical tensions on trade flows. According to the WTO (2023), trade flows between hypothetical geopolitical blocs based on foreign policy similarities have grown 4–6 percent less than trade within blocks since the onset of the war in Ukraine. According to the IMF terminology, the fall in trade and foreign direct investment has been more pronounced between rather than within these geopolitical blocs, a phenomenon they have even called a new "cold war" (Gopinath et al., 2024). In any case, according to this report, this fragmentation of the world economy is still relatively small. It should be noted that a significant portion of the trade

---

[29] See the most recent report in www.cpb.nl/en/world-trade-monitor-february-2024.

Table 3 Breakdown of active distortive industrial policy instruments

	Domestic subsidy	Export barrier	Export subsidy	FDI	Import barrier	Localization	Procurement
A. Developing countries versus advanced economies							
Developing countries	242	35	25	16	146	53	7
Advanced economies	788	69	148	9	111	124	33
B. By region							
Sub-Saharian Africa	6	2	1	0	3	1	0
South Asia	37	26	6	1	73	29	1
North America	209	20	26	4	21	55	22
Middle East and North Africa	7	0	1	0	3	0	0
Latin America and the Caribbean	84	7	11	3	104	13	0
Europe and Central Asia	427	47	53	14	68	5	13
Asia Pacific	148	40	55	6	278	15	2

Source: Evenett et al. (2024), Tables 4 and 5.

restrictions occurs between the United States, the European Union, and China. Despite being occasionally framed as national security issues, these restrictions may be more closely associated with economic tensions between the old economic powers and the rising Asian giant than to purely geopolitical factors. Furthermore, most developing countries from all regions are reluctant to be drawn into a "cold war" scenario, given the importance of their trade relations with all partners.

On the downside, it is important to underscore the weakening of the WTO dispute settlement mechanism. This decline stems from the United States' opposition to the nomination of new members of the Appellate Body since December 2017, resulting in the body being left without the minimum number of members to operate since December 2021. The primary reasons for that country's position were concerns that the Appellate Body was broadening the interpretation of the agreements, thus changing the rights and obligations of members, using its reports as legal precedents, and exhibiting inefficiency in meeting deadlines. This was, of course, unfortunate since this is possibly the best mechanism of its kind in international economic cooperation. It has been widely used by both developed and developing countries for trade disputes among themselves, and between the two blocs of countries. Due to the collapse of this body, the European Union members, who had been strong supporters of this mechanism, have joined other countries in using alternative dispute resolution processes.

On the positive side, it must be said that the world trade in services has sustained its upward trajectory, especially the exports of digitally delivered services, which have witnessed a more than threefold increase since 2005. This remarkable growth highlights the increasing importance of the digital economy in global trade. Additionally, trade in environmental goods has also grown equally fast, reflecting a rising global commitment to sustainable practices and green technologies (WTO, 2023). In institutional terms, it should be added that, since entering into force, the WTO's Trade Facilitation Agreement has also had positive effects on agricultural trade (see also WTO, 2023). Furthermore, it is worth mentioning that, after the significant disruptions caused by the COVID-19 pandemic on global value chains, they have experienced a recovery. However, this recovery comes with an element of "nearshoring," as well as the impacts of trade restrictions imposed by the United States and the European Union on China.

Also, we could highlight the promotion of regional and interregional trade agreements. On top of the agreements traditionally led by the European Union and the United States, China has emerged as the most active actor in this area in recent years, negotiating and signing numerous trade deals. Although these agreements can fragment global trade, they also promote freer trade within their regions. These regional and interregional trade agreements have been considered consistent with the WTO since the launch of this institution in 1995.

The 13th WTO Ministerial Conference in Abu Dhabi that took place in 2024 highlighted the continued importance of this organization as a platform for dialogue on trade issues among diverse nations. However, the Conference presented a mixed picture.[30] The most discouraging issue was that the deep trade restrictions were not on the agenda at all. In fact, given the strength of the problems generated by these policies, it can be argued that the WTO should work toward a new agreement on the limits of industrial policy, borrowing from the regulations on export subsidies under the current framework.

Some progress was made in reforming the WTO's dispute settlement system. While some issues regarding appeals, reviews, and accessibility remained unresolved, a draft outlining potential reforms was presented, and discussions will continue, hopefully having a functioning system very soon. This issue was not mentioned at all in the main Ministerial Declaration, although it was subject to a short Ministerial Decision.[31]

Another stalemate involved disagreements on updating agricultural trade rules. In particular, broad disagreements on public stockholding for food security purposes prevented any progress in this area. This issue relates to how governments buy, store, and distribute food reserves, ensuring availability for populations in need. They could not agree on whether net food exporting countries of specific goods should refrain from imposing export prohibitions or restrictions, particularly when those foodstuffs are imported by LDCs.

Several agricultural exporting countries also published a statement expressing their concern about the restrictive and potentially discriminatory effect of trade-related environmental measures recently adopted by WTO members – particularly by the European Union. They rejected the adoption of a unilateral approach to address global issues, as well as measures that create unjustified barriers to international trade. They also regretted the lack of clearer progress in the reforms of the agricultural trade agreement, which have been on the agenda for a long time. This includes discussions regarding subsidies to agriculture by the developed countries, which have been ongoing since the negotiations of the original WTO agreement.

A favorable development was that members recognized the importance of services to the global economy. The Conference saw the entry into force of new

---

[30] See the Ministerial Declaration in WTO (2024), and the press review in www.wto.org/english/news_e/news24_e/mc13_01mar24_e.htm. See also the reference to some of the other decisions in the next footnotes/.

[31] https://docs.wto.org/dol2fe/Pages/SS/directdoc.aspx?filename=q:/WT/MIN24/37.pdf&Open=True.

disciplines on domestic service regulations. These rules focus on licensing, qualifications, and technical standards, making it easier for businesses, especially small and women-owned ones, to navigate the regulatory environment.[32] This initiative is supported by seventy-two members, representing over 92 percent of global services trade. It is estimated that these regulations could potentially lead to annual cost reductions exceeding $125 billion.

In terms of trade facilitation, the moratorium on customs duties for e-commerce was extended, benefiting online businesses worldwide. Members also agreed to maintain the current practice of not imposing customs duties on electronic transmissions until the fourteenth session of the Ministerial Conference or March 31, 2026, whichever is earlier. This extension was approved despite strong opposition from some developing countries, particularly India, South Africa, and Indonesia, which highlighted their concerns about potential impacts of this rule on their domestic industries.

Additionally, ministers representing 123 WTO members adopted the Investment Facilitation for Development (IFD) Agreement and made it available to the public. This initiative, promoted since the spring of 2017 by a coalition of developing and least-developed WTO members, seeks to enhance the investment climate, streamline business procedures, and facilitate opportunities for investors across all sectors. The countries that adopted the agreement represent three-quarters of the WTO membership, including ninety developing economies and twenty-six LDCs.

Sustainability also emerged as a prominent theme, highlighting WTO's potential role in fostering environmentally conscious trade practices. Specifically, there was notable progress on initiatives addressing plastic pollution, environmental trade policies, and fossil fuel subsidies. Additionally, the acceptance of the Fisheries Subsidies Agreement, aimed at curbing harmful fishing subsidies, continued to gain momentum, with the total number of WTO members formally accepting the Agreement reaching seventy-one.

Ministers adopted Ministerial Decisions reviewing the mandate of special and differential treatment provisions for developing and LDCs to make them more precise, effective, and operational.[33] They also agreed on concrete measures to ease the path to graduation from the category of LDCs. This was a central issue in the main Ministerial Declaration and responds also to the recurrent call by the United Nations Committee for Development Policy to guarantee good trade benefits for LDCs, as well as transitory ones for countries that graduate from that status (CDP, 2021, chapter II). Two least-developed countries,

---

[32] www.wto.org/english/news_e/news24_e/serv_27feb24_e.htm.
[33] https://docs.wto.org/dol2fe/Pages/SS/directdoc.aspx?filename=q:/WT/MIN24/36.pdf&Open=True.

Comoros and Timor-Leste, became WTO members, marking the first new additions in almost a decade.

Commodity exchange reform is an issue that has been overlooked in global debates but could significantly impact the financing of sustainable development – particularly for the large number of developing countries that are dependent on the exports of these goods. These exchanges, which have operated much the same since the late nineteenth century, are privately owned and serve as intermediaries for the bulk of primary commodities. In these exchanges, producing countries are de facto price-takers, and their vulnerability has been significantly exacerbated by the expansion of the financialization of commodity markets. This has resulted in unpredictable booms and busts, disproportionately benefiting asset owners, consumers, and intermediaries, while contributing to poverty and inequality in developing countries.

While commodity exchanges play a crucial role in global commodity trading by providing liquidity, price discovery, and risk management tools, they also pose significant concerns. A major one is the potential for market manipulation. Large traders or speculative investors may employ strategic trading practices, such as cornering the market or spreading rumors, to create artificial demand or supply shocks, leading to price volatility and windfall profits. This volatility disproportionately affects producers in developing countries reliant on commodity exports and consumers facing unpredictable price fluctuations. Moreover, a lack of transparency in operations, pricing mechanisms, and decision-making processes within commodity exchanges fosters suspicions of insider trading and market rigging, exacerbating inequalities in market access. In fact, an important issue in regulation is the dichotomy between the regulatory issues that commodity trades have as commercial and manufacturing firms and their unregulated financial activities, which also contrasts with the extensive regulations of other financial activities.[34]

The impact of commodity exchange dynamics is particularly severe on small-scale producers in agriculture and some mineral sectors. Fluctuating prices driven by speculative activities disrupt these producers' livelihoods, stability, and investment decisions. Additionally, commodity exchanges are also criticized for incentivizing unsustainable production practices and environmental degradation, posing challenges to long-term sustainability goals. The regulatory landscape surrounding commodity exchanges also faces scrutiny, with concerns raised about inadequate oversight, regulatory loopholes, and lax enforcement, which can lead to market abuses and systemic risks.

---

[34] On these issues and commodity markets in general, see UNCTAD (2024), chapter III.

Addressing these criticisms requires comprehensive reforms within commodity exchange systems. Initiatives to enhance transparency, implement robust regulatory measures, promote responsible trading practices, and prioritize SDGs are imperative. Collaborative efforts involving governments, regulators, industry stakeholders, and civil society are essential to foster fair, transparent, and resilient commodity markets that benefit all participants and contribute positively to global economic stability and sustainability.

It is also important to increase the participation of producing countries in the markets for the manufactured goods that process the commodities they export, thereby ensuring a more substantial share in the relevant value chains. This requires a system of import tariffs in the consuming countries where the processed goods are taxed at a similar rate as the primary commodities. This would incentivize processing activities to take place in producing countries. Furthermore, there should be financing mechanisms to promote the participation of firms from producing countries in the marketing and manufacturing of goods in the consuming countries.

Price instability poses a significant challenge across all commodities: consequently, the establishment of buffer stocks to cushion sharp price fluctuations, which could include international virtual or physical buffer stocks for important commodities, and particularly for important food products, benefitting both producers and consumers (Weber and Schulken, 2024). Stabilization funds to support producers in the countries of origin of those goods would be an important complement. This is particularly important for peasants and small firms in those countries, who would also benefit from market mechanisms ensuring they can sell at a guaranteed price. Currently, international commodity agreements do not play an important role in determining commodity prices – except in the case of oil. However, such agreements can facilitate dialogue among producing and consuming countries, as well as producing countries with private firms that have an important role in those markets. The International Coffee Agreement is an important case in this regard, but this practice should be extended to other commodity markets.

6 Critical Institutional Issues

The institutional issues that the international financial system reform must address are basically three. The first is to continue expanding the voice and participation of developing countries in the Bretton Woods institutions. The second is to evolve toward a more representative government at the top of the international economic cooperation system. The third is a denser architecture, which should include more regional institutions. The possibilities for progress in these reforms are diverse and now face the effects of current geopolitical rivalries, which limit the ability to agree on global solutions.

In the case of the Bretton Woods organizations, the first issue is to reform the composition of the capital contributions or quotas of the member countries. Added to this is the structure through which decisions are made, which is related to the role that ministerial bodies, executive boards, and administration have in the decisions of these organizations. No less important is the need for open election system of the Managing Director of the IMF and the President of the World Bank, in which citizens of any member state could participate.

In terms of representation, it is essential to update the formulas that determine the contributions of the organizations, taking into account the relative size of the economies. The second is the weight of the basic votes. It is worth remembering in this regard that the Bretton Woods agreements agreed on these votes, which are the same for all countries, but they lost importance over time. The total votes of countries are also reflected in the composition of the seats on the executive boards of the organizations. To these issues we can add the convenience of using the double majority system more widely, which would favor developing countries, as they have a larger number of members. And, no less important, it is important to eliminate the veto power for decisions that require 85 percent of votes to be approved, which is an advantage that the United States has but that a small group of countries with high capital participation can potentially exercise.

Regarding capital contributions, the most important element is the overrepresentation of Europe and the underrepresentation of Asia, as a reflection of the significant changes that the world economy has experienced over several decades, which have not been clearly recognized in these organizations. In the case of the IMF, the reform carried out in 2008–10 meant that developed countries, especially European ones, lost about 4 percent of the quota in favor of developing countries.[35] The increase in capital from developing countries favored China and some other countries, including Brazil, the Republic of Korea, India, Mexico, and Turkey, but there were also losers, including Argentina, Venezuela, and, especially, as a bloc, the low-income countries. The increase in basic votes generated a slightly more reasonable decision: Europeans lost more to developing countries, but especially low-income countries increased their voting power.

In the case of the World Bank, the 2008 reform increased the basic votes and gave an additional chair to Africa, and the 2010 reform changed the capital composition. As a result of both, the share of developing and transition

---

[35] There were, however, some European winners, including Spain and Ireland.

countries in voting power in the IBRD increased from 42.6 percent to 47.19 percent. The criterion of gradually equalizing the voting power of developing and transition countries was also accepted, but no additional steps have been taken in this regard. In IDA, which supports the poorest notions, the power of developed countries, especially European ones, remained higher due to the inclusion of contribution to development as one of the criteria to determine the capital shares, since these countries are large international donors.

The IMF's system of quota contributions is once again a subject of debate – though for a decision that would take place in 2025 – but not yet that of the IBRD. However, in both cases the possibility of significant additional changes in the composition of said capital contributions is unlikely, largely due to the considerable gain that China would have in relation to developed countries.[36] An alternative that the UN has suggested is to increase again the basic votes, to bring them to the level they had when these organizations were created in Bretton Woods (United Nations, 2023b, Action 1).[37]

The issue of the power of the different decision-making bodies is related, first of all, to the fact that the agreements reached in the ministerial meetings – the International Monetary and Financial Committee and the Development Committee – which are held two times a year, are not decisions but recommendations to the executive committees, which are those who have the said power, a rule that many consider inappropriate. Furthermore, some analysts have pointed out that the heads of these organizations can make decisions on issues that should correspond to the executive committees, an issue that seems particularly important in the case of the World Bank. These are areas that have been the subject of controversy, but there have been no agreements to modify them.

Regarding the need for an open and transparent system of electing the heads of the IMF and the World Bank, the first thing that must be highlighted is the need to respect the principle of equal treatment of all member countries in their aspiration to direct international entities, a principle that is clearly in force in other organizations of the United Nations' system. In the case of the IMF, it can be noted that there is at least competition among European countries in the appointment of its head, which has led to important changes, including the election of its current managing director, from Bulgaria, a minority country of Europe. In the case of the World Bank, the only semi-competitive process was that of 2012, in which there were two candidates from developing countries proposed by the G24, the group that represents these countries in the Bretton

---

[36] In the current discussions on IMF quotas, a proposal that has a high level of acceptance is to protect the quota of low-income countries that have access to the *Poverty Reduction and Growth Trust*.

[37] In the case of the IMF, it would increase from 5.5% to one-ninth of the total votes.

Woods organizations, wanting to establish the principle that the election of the heads of these organizations must be open. As expected, given the agreement between Europe and the United States to divide the management of these two financial organizations between them, the candidate from the United States was elected. There has been no competition in the subsequent processes – the reelection of the president of the World Bank in 2016 and the election of new presidents in 2019 and 2023.

The second key institutional issue, having a representative committee at the top of the international economic cooperation system, is also a recommendation the UN has made in one of its recent reports (United Nations, 2023b). This recommendation is part of a long history of proposals based on the creation of institutions such as an Economic Security Council or an L27 based on the current ECOSOC of the United Nations (Rosenthal, 2007; Dervis, 2005, chapter 3). These proposals seek to address the inherent challenges of global economic governance by advocating for a more inclusive decision-making body that reflects the diverse economic interests and priorities of all member states.

The most interesting proposal was the one made by the Commission of Experts on Reforms of the International Financial and Monetary System, convened by the UN General Assembly after the North Atlantic crisis, better known as the Stiglitz Commission: that of creating a Coordination Council Global Economic (United Nations, 2009, chapter 4). According to this proposal, this Council would serve as a coordination instrument of the UN *system*, which includes all specialized agencies, including the IMF and the World Bank, as well as the World Trade Organization, which should be integrated into the system. It would have a representation regime based on constituencies and weighted voting, as in the Bretton Woods organizations, and would operate as a Council at the level of first leaders, as is the case today with the G20, which could in turn convene ministerial meetings on specific issues.

A council of this type would help coordinate different organizations and identify existing gaps in the current cooperation system. It could make recommendations to specialized agencies on the issues within their jurisdictions, but it would leave the relevant decisions and actions in their hands. For its part, although the weighted vote would generate resistance among countries that defend the principle of "one country, one vote" inherent to the United Nations, it would recognize the fact that a global economic government system cannot function if it does not give special weight to the most powerful actors, which requires their presence at the negotiating table; otherwise, they would simply tend to ignore the decisions of the corresponding body. In any case, the specific mechanism adopted for its composition should overcome the deficiencies in the representation of countries that characterize the Bretton Woods institutions.

Some of these proposals are similar to those of the Palais Royal Initiative (2011), which proposed a governance structure for the world economy at three levels, although limited to the international monetary system, and therefore with less scope than the council proposed by the Stiglitz Commission. For its part, one of the recent United Nations reports proposes a top body that would meet biennially at the level of heads of government, which would include members of the G20 and the ECOSOC, the Secretary General of the UN, and the heads of international financial organizations (United Nations, 2023b, Action 2).

It should be noted that in any scheme the United Nations must retain an important role in the governance of the global economy. Its General Assembly, the summits it convenes, and ECOSOC have demonstrated their effectiveness as mechanisms for consensus building. In the sphere of international finance, its history includes the sequence of three United Nations Conferences on Financing for Development, from Monterrey in 2002 to Addis Ababa in 2015, with the fourth taking place in Spain in 2025. The global environmental agenda and many other international agendas are also products of the dialogues and decisions adopted at the United Nations. The organization has also been key in agreements on global development goals, especially the SDGs adopted in 2015. If a new apex body is created, ECOSOC could continue to function as coordinator of the economic, social, and environmental activities of the United Nations *organizations* (the UN secretariat, funds and programs), but not the UN *system*.

If a new top organization is created, it would overcome the "elite multilateralism," which has been historically constituted by the sequence of the G10, the G7, and the G20. The latter, organized at the level of heads of state after the North Atlantic financial crisis, has had advantages and disadvantages. The most important advantage is that it is more representative than the G7. However, as its predecessor, it is an ad hoc self-appointed body with representation problems and a strange relationship with international organizations in which the countries that participate in these bodies are also members. The G20 had an important initial leadership, but later he weakened. Furthermore, deep geopolitical divisions among its members now limit their ability to act. In fact, as we pointed out in Ocampo and Stiglitz (2011), the Stiglitz Commission proposal could be understood as making the G20 a United Nations institution, but with an election of its members, which should include the possibility that smaller countries could be able to be active participants.

The third family of institutional issues include the reforms of the MDBs and the IMF, as argued in the first two sections of this Element, but also, crucially, stronger organizations in the areas of debt restructuring, international tax cooperation, and global trade. In debt the world needs to create a permanent institutional mechanism to restructure sovereign debts and a global asset registry. In tax cooperation, the best reform would be to transform the UN Committee of Experts on International Cooperation in Tax Matters into an intergovernmental organ, and to strengthen the UN Secretariat in a parallel way to work with the OECD in a complementary way. In trade, the world needs to reestablish the dispute settlement mechanism but also stronger action by WTO to manage the massive trade interventions that have been put in place by major countries in recent years.

It is also essential in all areas to develop a strong multilevel architecture – thus recognizing that globalization is also a world of open regionalism. This means that there is potential complementarity between regional and global entities, as well as competition between them, which is also healthy. An additional virtue of an architecture of this type is a federalist type of argument: the strong sense of belonging of medium and small countries to regional institutions, since they have a very limited voice in the global ones. A consequence of this is that the actions of regional institutions respond more strongly to their interests.

As pointed out throughout this Element, an architecture of this type already exists in the case of MDBs, which can undoubtedly continue to improve, but should be extended in particular to the international monetary system and international tax cooperation, where these networks are half empty. For this reason, creating a broader group of regional monetary organizations and regional tax cooperation bodies should be one of the priorities of international financial reform.

References

Brookings Institution (2024), *Reforms for a 21st Century International Financial Architecture: Independent Expert Reflections on the United Nations "Our Comon Agenda,"* Washington DC, April.

CDP (United Nations Committee for Development Policy) (2021), *Handbook of the Least Developed Countries Category: Inclusion, Graduation and Special Support Measures*, 4th ed., October.

CLAAF (Comité Latino Americano de Asuntos Financieros) (2023), "A Proposal for the IMF: A New Instrument of International Liquidity Provision for EMDEs," December 11, https://claaf.org/wp-content/uploads/2023/12/claaf-statement-special-report-EMF.pdf.

Climate Bonds Initiative (2022), *Sustainable Debt Global State of the Market 2022*, www.climatebonds.net/files/reports/cbi_sotm_2022_03e.pdf.

CPI (Climate Policy Initiative) (2023), "An Innovative IFI Operating Model for the 21st Century," www.climatepolicyinitiative.org/wp-content/uploads/2023/06/CPI_An-Innovative-IFI-Operating-Model-for-the-21st-Century_updated.pdf.

Dervis, Kemal (2005), *A Better Globalization, Legitimacy, Governance and Reform*, Washington DC: Brookings Institution Press.

Development Initiatives (2023), *Climate Vulnerability, Climate Finance (ODA) and Protracted Crisis*, https://devinit.org/resources/climate-finance-vulnerability-crisis/.

Eichengreen, Barry. (2008), *Globalizing Capital: A History of the International Monetary System*, New Jersey: Princeton University Press.

Eichengreen, Barry (2011), *Exorbitant Privilege: The Rise and Fall of the Dollar and the Future of the International Monetary System*, Oxford: Oxford University Press.

EU Tax Observatory (2024), *Global Tax Evasion Report 2024*, www.taxobservatory.eu//www-site/uploads/2023/10/global_tax_evasion_report_24.pdf.

Evenett, Simon, Adam Jakubik, Fernando Martín and Michele Ruta (2024), "The Return of Industrial Policy in Data," *IMF Working Paper WP/24/1*, Washington DC: International Monetary Fund, January.

G20 (Group of 20) 2009, "Declaration on Delivering Resources through the International Financial Institutions." London, April 2.

G20 (2022), *Boosting MDB's Investment Capacity*, An Independent Review of Multilateral Development Banks' Capital Adequacy Frameworks.

G20 (2023a), *Strengthening Multilateral Development Banks: The Triple Agenda*, Report of a Group of the Independent Experts Group, Volumes 1 and 2, June and September.

G20 (2023b), "G20 New Delhi Declaration," September 10, www.mea.gov.in/Images/CPV/G20-New-Delhi-Leaders-Declaration.pdf.

G24 (Group of 24) (2019), "Working Group on Tax Policy and International Tax Cooperation: Proposal for Addressing Tax Challenges Arising from Digitalisation," www.g24.org/wp-content/uploads/2019/03/G-24_proposal_for_Taxation_of_Digital_Economy_Jan17_Special_Session_2.pdf.

G24 (2020), "Comments of the G24 on the Ongoing Work under G20/OECD Inclusive Framework under BEPS on the Work for Addressing Tax Challenges Arising from the Digitalisation under Pillar One and Pillar Two," www.g24.org/wp-content/uploads/2020/08/Comments-of-the-G-24-to-Steering-Group-April-2020_22.04.pdf.

G24 (2023), "Communiqué," April 11, www.g24.org/wp-content/uploads/2023/04/English_G-24-Communique-Final_-Spring-2023.pdf.

Gallagher, Kevin, Rishikesh Ram Bhandary, Rebecca Ray and Luma Ramos (2023), "Reforming Bretton Woods Institutions to Achieve Climate Change and Development Goals," *One Earth 6*, October 20.

Global Sovereign Debt Roundtable (2024), "2nd Cochairs Progress Report," April 17, www.imf.org/-/media/Files/Miscellaneous/gsdr-cochairs-progress-report-april-2024.ashx.

Gopinath, Gita, Pierre-Olivier Gourinchas, Andrea F. Presbitero and Petia Topalova (2024), "Changing Global Linkages: A New Cold War?, IMF Working Paper WP/2476, Washington DC: International Monetary Fund.

GRI (Global Reporting Initiative) (2021), "GRI 207: Tax 2019," available at www.globalreporting.org.

Griffith-Jones, Stephany and José Antonio Ocampo, eds. (2018), *The Future of National Development Banks*, Oxford: Oxford University Press.

Hagan, Sean (2005), "Designing a Legal Framework to Restructure Sovereign Debt," *Georgetown Journal of International Law*, 36(2): 299–402.

ICRICT (Independent Commission for the Reform of International Corporate Taxation) (2022a), "It Is Time for a Global Asset Registry to Tackle Hidden Wealth," www.icrict.com/.

ICRICT (2022b), "An Emergency Tax Plan to Confront the Inflation Crisis," September, www.icrict.com/.

ICRICT (2024a), "ICRICT Letter to the Ad-Hoc Committee to Draft Terms of Reference for a UN Framework Convention on International Tax Cooperation," March 15. www.icrict.com/.

ICRICT (2024b), "ICRICT Statement in Response to the Chair's Request to Provide Written Comments on the Bureau's Proposal for the Zero Draft Terms of Reference for a United Nations Framework Convention on International Tax Cooperation," June 7, www.icrict.com/.

IMF (International Monetary Fund) (2011), "Enhancing International Monetary Stability–A Role for the SDR?" January 7. Washington, DC: Strategy, Policy, and Review Department, January 7.

IMF (2012), "The Liberalization and Management of Capital Flows: An Institutional View," November 14.

IMF (2020), "The International Architecture for Resolving Sovereign Debt Crises Involving Private-Sector Creditors: Recent Developments, Challenges, and Reform Options," September 23.

IMF (2022), *Global Financial Stability Report*, October.

IMF (2023a), *World Economic Outlook: A Rocky Recovery*, April.

IMF (2023b), "Review of the Flexible Credit Line, the Short-Term Liquidity Line, and the Precautionary and Liquidity Line, and Proposals for Reform," *IMF Policy Paper*, October.

IMF-IEO (Independent Evaluations Office) (2024), "The Evolving Application of the IMF's Mandate," Evaluation Report, https://ieo.imf.org/en/our-work/Evaluations/Completed/2024-0618-evolving-application-of-the-imfs-mandate.

Kenen, Peter (2010), "An SDR-Based Reserve System," *Journal of Globalization and Development*, 1(2): Article 13.

Kharas, Homi and Amar Battacharya (2023), "The Trillion-Dollar Bank: Making IBRD Fit for Purpose in the 21st Century," *Working Paper 181*, Brookings Institution, April, www.brookings.edu/wp-content/uploads/2023/04/KharasBhattacharya-2023.pdf.

Krueger, Anne O. (2002), *A New Approach to Sovereign Debt Restructuring*, Washington, DC: International Monetary Fund.

MDBs (Multilateral Development Banks) (2022), *2021 Joint Report on Multilateral Development Banks' Climate Finance*, October, www.eib.org/attachments/lucalli/mdbs_joint_report_2021_en.pdf.

Mühlich, Laurissa and Marina Zucker-Marques (2023), "Closing the Global Crisis Finance Gap," *GEGI Policy Brief 025*, Boston University Global Development Policy Center, July.

Neunuebel, Carolyn, Valerie Laxton and Hayden Higgins (2023), *How Multilateral Development Banks Can Use Policy-Based Financing to Support Climate-Resilient Economies*, World Resources Institute, February 17, www.wri.org/technical-perspectives/multilateral-development-banks-policy-based-financing.

Ocampo, José Antonio (2017), *Resetting the International Monetary (Non) System*, Oxford and Helsinki: Oxford University Press and UNU-WIDER.

Ocampo, José Antonio (2022), "A Pandemic of Debt," *Project Syndicate*, December 12.

Ocampo, José Antonio and Joseph Stiglitz (2011), "From the G-20 to a Global Economic Coordination Council," *Journal of Globalization and Development*, 2(2), Article 9.

Ocampo, José Antonio and Victor Ortega (2022), "The Global Development Banks' Architecture," *Review of Political Economy*, 34(2): 224–248.

Ocampo José Antonio and Karla Daniela González (2024), "Financing International Public Goods: The Role of MDBs and Development Assistance," *Working Paper* 2024/01, Initiative for Policy Dialogue, Columbia University, https://policydialogue.org/publications/working-papers/financing-international-public-goods-the-role-of-mdbs-and-development-assistance/.

OECD (Organisation for Economic Cooperation and Development) (2016), "Multilateral Convention to Implement Tax Treaty Related Measures to Prevent BEPS," www.oecd.org/tax/treaties/multilateral-convention-to-implement-tax-treaty-related-measures-to-prevent-BEPS.pdf.

OECD (2023) "Biodiversity and Development Finance 2015–2021 Progress towards Target 19 of the Kunming-Montreal Global Biodiversity Framework," https://one.oecd.org/document/DCD(2023)49/en/pdf.

OECD (2024), "Climate-Related Official Development Assistance in 2021: A Snapshot," https://one.oecd.org/document/DCD(2024)20/en/pdf#:~:text=Official%20development%20assistance%20(ODA)%20with,30.6%25%20over%202020%2D21.

Ostry, Jonathan Ostry, Atish Ghosh, Marcos Chamon and Mahvash Qureshi (2012), "Tools for Managing Financial-Stability Risks from Capital Inflows," *Journal of International Economics*, 88(2): 407–421.

Palais Royal Initiative (2011), "Reform of the International Monetary System: A Cooperative Approach for the 21st Century," in Jack T. Boorman and André Icard (eds), *Reform of the International Monetary System: The Palais Royal Initiative*, New Delhi: Sage, chapter 2.

Rivetti, Diego (2022), "Achieving Comparability of Treatment under the G20's Common Framework," World Bank, https://documents.worldbank.org/en/publication/documents-reports/documentdetail/426641645456786855/achieving-comparability-of-treatment-under-the-g20-s-common-framework.

Rosenthal, Gert (2007), "The Economic and Social Council of the United Nations," in Thomas G. Weiss and Sam Daws (eds), *The Oxford Handbook on the United Nations*, New York: Oxford University Press, chapter 7, pp. 165–177.

References

Songwe, Vera, Nicholas Stern and Amar Bhattacharya (2022), "Finance for Climate Action: Scaling up Investment for Climate and Development," London: Grantham Research Institute on Climate Change and the Environment, London School of Economics and Political Science, November.

TCDIMF (Task Force on Climate, Development and the International Monetary Fund) (2023), *"The International Monetary Fund Climate and Development: A Preliminary Assessment,"* Boston University Global Development Policy Center, March.

UNCTAD (United Nations Conference on Trade and Development) (2024), *Trade and Development Report 2023*, Geneva: UNCTAD.

UN (United Nations) (2009), *Report of the Commission of Experts Convened of the President of the UN General Assembly on Reforms of the International Monetary and Financial System* (Stiglitz Commission), September 21.

UN (2015), "The Addis Ababa Action Agenda," https://sustainabledevelopment.un.org/frameworks/addisababaactionagenda.

UN (2022), "Credit Rating Agencies and Sovereign Debt: Four Proposals to Support Achievement of the SDGs," Policy Brief No. 131, United Nations Department of Economic and Social Affairs, March, www.un-ilibrary.org/content/papers/10.18356/27081990-131/read.

UN (2023a), "United Nations Secretary-General SDG Stimulus to Deliver Agenda 2030," *Report of the Secretary-General*, February.

UN (2023b), "United Nations, Reforms to the International Financial Architecture, Our Common Agenda," *Policy Brief 6*, May.

UN (2023c), "Promotion of Inclusive and Effective Tax Cooperation at the United Nations," *Report of the Secretary-General*, July.

UN (2023d), *Political Declaration of the High-Level Political Forum on Sustainable Development Convened under the Auspices of the General Assembly*, September.

UN (2024a), *Financing for Sustainable Development Report 2024: Financing for Development at a Crossroads*.

UN (2024b), "Economic and Social Council Forum on Financing for Development Follow-Up," April 25.

UN (2024c), "Chair's Proposal for Draft Terms of Reference for a United Nations Framework Convention on International Tax Cooperation, August 15 https://financing.desa.un.org/sites/default/files/2024-08/Chair%27s%20proposal%20draft%20ToR_L.4_15%20Aug%202024____.pdf.

UN (2024d), *Pact for the Future*, September, www.un.org/sites/un2.un.org/files/sotf-pact_for_the_future_adopted.pdf.

UNFCC (United Nations Framework Convention on Climate Change) (2022), "COP26 Outcomes: Finance for Climate Adaptation," https://unfccc.int/pro

cess-and-meetings/the-paris-agreement/the-glasgow-climate-pact/cop26-out comes-finance-for-climate-adaptation.

Volz, Ulrich, Shamshad Akhtar, Kevin P. Gallagher, Stephany Griffith-Jones, Jörg Haas and Moritz Kraemer (2021), "Debt Relief for a Green and Inclusive Recovery: Securing Private-Sector Participation and Creating Policy Space for Sustainable Development." Berlin, London, and Boston: Heinrich-Böll-Stiftung; SOAS, University of London; and Boston University https://drgr.org/files/2021/06/DRGR-Report-2021-Securing-Private-Sector-Participation.pdf.

Weber, Isabella and Merle Schulken (2024), "Towards a Post-neoliberal Stabilization Paradigm for an Age of Overlapping Emergencies: Revising International Buffer Stocks Based on the Case of Food," *Working Paper* No. 602, Political Economy Research Institute, University of Massachusetts Amherst, https://peri.umass.edu/?view=article&id=1816:towards-a-post-neoliberal-stabilization-paradigm-for-an-age-of-overlapping-emergencies-revisiting-international-buffer-stocks-based-on-the-case-of-food&catid=10.

Wier, Ludvig and Gabriel Zucman (2023), "Global Profit Shifting 1975-2019," *Working Paper*, EU Tax Observatory.

Williamson, John (2009). "*Understanding Special Drawing Rights (SDRs).*" Policy Brief PB09-11, June. Washington, DC: Peter G. Peterson Institute for International Economics.

World Bank (2022a), "Debt Service Suspension Initiative," March 11, www.worldbank.org/en/topic/debt/brief/covid-19-debt-service-suspension-initiative.

World Bank (2022b), *World Development Report 2022: Finance for an Equitable Recovery*, Washington DC: World Bank.

World Bank (2022b), "Evolving the World Bank Group's Mission, Operations, and Resources: A Roadmap," December.

World Bank (2023a), *International Debt Report 2023*, Washington DC: World Bank.

World Bank (2023b), "Ending Poverty on a Livable Planet: Report to Governors on World Bank Evolution," Document Presented to the Development Committee, September 28.

World Bank (2024), "From Vision to Impact: Implementing the World Bank Group Evolution," Document Presented to the Development Committee, March 29.

WTO (World Trade Organization) (2023), *World Trade Report 2023: Re-globalization for a Secure, Inclusive and Sustainable Future*, Geneva: WTO.

WTO (2024), Abu Dhabi Ministerial Declaration, March 4, https://docs.wto.org/dol2fe/Pages/SS/directdoc.aspx?filename=q:/WT/MIN24/DEC.pdf&Open=True.

Zucker-Marques, Marina, Ulrich Volz and Kevin P. Gallagher (2023), "Debt Relief By Multilateral Lenders. Why, How and How Much?" Boston, London, Berlin: Boston University Global Development Policy Center; Centre for Sustainable Finance, SOAS, University of London; Heinrich-Böll-Stiftung https://drgr.org/files/2023/09/DRGR-Report-2023-Digital-FINAL.pdf.

Zucman, Gabriel (2024), "A Blueprint for a Coordinated Minimum Effective Taxation Standard for Ultra-High-Net-Worth Individuals," Report Commissioned by the Brazilian G20 Presidency, http://gabriel-zucman.eu/files/report-g20.pdf.

Cambridge Elements

Development Economics

Series Editor-in-Chief
Kunal Sen
UNU-WIDER and University of Manchester

Kunal Sen, UNU-WIDER Director, is Editor-in-Chief of the Cambridge Elements in Development Economics series. Professor Sen has over three decades of experience in academic and applied development economics research, and has carried out extensive work on international finance, the political economy of inclusive growth, the dynamics of poverty, social exclusion, female labour force participation, and the informal sector in developing economies. His research has focused on India, East Asia, and sub-Saharan Africa.

In addition to his work as Professor of Development Economics at the University of Manchester, Kunal has been the Joint Research Director of the Effective States and Inclusive Development (ESID) Research Centre, and a Research Fellow at the Institute for Labor Economics (IZA). He has also served in advisory roles with national governments and bilateral and multilateral development agencies, including the UK's Department for International Development, Asian Development Bank, and the International Development Research Centre.

Thematic Editors
Tony Addison
University of Copenhagen and UNU-WIDER

Tony Addison is a Professor of Economics in the University of Copenhagen's Development Economics Research Group. He is also a Non-Resident Senior Research Fellow at UNU-WIDER, Helsinki, where he was previously the Chief Economist-Deputy Director. In addition, he is Professor of Development Studies at the University of Manchester. His research interests focus on the extractive industries, energy transition, and macroeconomic policy for development.

Chris Barrett
SC Johnson College of Business, Cornell University

Chris Barrett is an agricultural and development economist at Cornell University. He is the Stephen B. and Janice G. Ashley Professor of Applied Economics and Management; and International Professor of Agriculture at the Charles H. Dyson School of Applied Economics and Management. He is also an elected Fellow of the American Association for the Advancement of Science, the Agricultural and Applied Economics Association, and the African Association of Agricultural Economists.

Carlos Gradín
University of Vigo

Carlos Gradín is a professor of applied economics at the University of Vigo. His main research interest is the study of inequalities, with special attention to those that exist between population groups (e.g., by race or sex). His publications have contributed to improving the empirical evidence in developing and developed countries, as well as globally, and to improving the available data and methods used.

Rachel M. Gisselquist
UNU-WIDER

Rachel M. Gisselquist is a Senior Research Fellow and member of the Senior Management Team of UNU-WIDER. She specializes in the comparative politics of developing countries, with particular attention to issues of inequality, ethnic and identity politics, foreign aid and state building, democracy and governance, and sub-Saharan African politics. Dr Gisselquist has edited a dozen collections in these areas, and her articles are published in a range of leading journals.

Shareen Joshi
Georgetown University

Shareen Joshi is an Associate Professor of International Development at Georgetown University's School of Foreign Service in the United States. Her research focuses on issues of inequality, human capital investment and grassroots collective action in South Asia. Her work has been published in the fields of development economics, population studies, environmental studies and gender studies.

Patricia Justino
UNU-WIDER and IDS – UK

Patricia Justino is a Senior Research Fellow at UNU-WIDER and Professorial Fellow at the Institute of Development Studies (IDS) (on leave). Her research focuses on the relationship between political violence, governance and development outcomes. She has published widely in the fields of development economics and political economy and is the co-founder and co-director of the Households in Conflict Network (HiCN).

Marinella Leone
University of Pavia

Marinella Leone is an assistant professor at the Department of Economics and Management, University of Pavia, Italy. She is an applied development economist. Her more recent research focuses on the study of early child development parenting programmes, on education,and gender-based violence. In previous research she investigated the short-, long-term and intergenerational impact of conflicts on health, education and domestic violence. She has published in top journals in economics and development economics.

Jukka Pirttilä
University of Helsinki and UNU-WIDER

Jukka Pirttilä is Professor of Public Economics at the University of Helsinki and VATT Institute for Economic Research. He is also a Non-Resident Senior Research Fellow at UNU-WIDER. His research focuses on tax policy, especially for developing countries. He is a co-principal investigator at the Finnish Centre of Excellence in Tax Systems Research.

Andy Sumner
King's College London and UNU-WIDER

Andy Sumner is Professor of International Development at King's College London; a Non-Resident Senior Fellow at UNU-WIDER and a Fellow of the Academy of Social Sciences. He has published extensively in the areas of poverty, inequality, and economic development.

About the Series

Cambridge Elements in Development Economics is led by UNU-WIDER in partnership with Cambridge University Press. The series publishes authoritative studies on important topics in the field covering both micro and macro aspects of development economics.

United Nations University World Institute for Development Economics Research

United Nations University World Institute for Development Economics Research (UNU-WIDER) provides economic analysis and policy advice aiming to promote sustainable and equitable development for all. The institute began operations in 1985 in Helsinki, Finland, as the first research centre of the United Nations University. Today, it is one of the world's leading development economics think tanks, working closely with a vast network of academic researchers and policy makers, mostly based in the Global South.

Cambridge Elements

Development Economics

Elements in the Series

The 1918–20 Influenza Pandemic: A Retrospective in the Time of COVID-19
Prema-chandra Athukorala and Chaturica Athukorala

Parental Investments and Children's Human Capital in Low-to-Middle-Income Countries
Jere R. Behrman

Great Gatsby and the Global South: Intergenerational Mobility, Income Inequality, and Development
Diding Sakri, Andy Sumner and Arief Anshory Yusuf

Varieties of Structural Transformation: Patterns, Determinants, and Consequences
Kunal Sen

Economic Transformation and Income Distribution in China over Three Decades
Cai Meng, Bjorn Gustafsson and John Knight

Chilean Economic Development under Neoliberalism: Structural Transformation, High Inequality and Environmental Fragility
Andrés Solimano and Gabriela Zapata-Román

Hierarchy of Needs and the Measurement of Poverty and Standards of Living
Joseph Deutsch and Jacques Silber

New Structural Financial Economics: A Framework for Rethinking the Role of Finance in Serving the Real Economy
Justin Yifu Lin, Jiajun Xu, Zirong Yang and Yilin Zhang

Knowledge and Global Inequality Since 1800: Interrogating the Present as History
Dev Nathan

Survival of the Greenest: Economic Transformation in a Climate-conscious World
Amir Lebdioui

Escaping Poverty Traps and Unlocking Prosperity in the Face of Climate Risk: Lessons from Index-Based Livestock Insurance
Nathaniel D. Jensen, Francesco P. Fava, Andrew G. Mude, Christopher B. Barrett, Brenda Wandera-Gache, Anton Vrieling, Masresha Taye, Kazushi Takahashi, Felix Lung, Munenobu Ikegami, Polly Ericksen, Philemon Chelanga, Sommarat Chantarat, Michael Carter, Hassan Bashir and Rupsha Banerjee

Financing for Development: The Global Agenda
José Antonio Ocampo

A full series listing is available at: www.cambridge.org/CEDE

For EU product safety concerns, contact us at Calle de José Abascal, 56–1°,
28003 Madrid, Spain or eugpsr@cambridge.org.